# CRYPTOGRAPHY

## THE SCIENCE OF SECRET WRITING

By LAURENCE DWIGHT SMITH

NEW YORK
DOVER PUBLICATIONS, INC.

This Dover edition, first published in 1955, is an unabridged and corrected republication of the work originally published by W. W. Norton and Company in 1943.

*Library of Congress Catalog Card Number: 55-4373*
*International Standard Book Number*
*ISBN-13: 978-0-486-20247-1*
*ISBN-10: 0-486-20247-X*

Manufactured in the United States by Courier Corporation
20247X23 2014
www.doverpublications.com

## *Contents*

Virtues of perfect ciphers: "... that they be not laborious to write and read; that they be impossible to decipher; and, in some cases, that they be without suspicion." — *Francis Bacon*

# *Preface*

It is the purpose of this book to present the fundamentals of secret communication concisely and simply. The first section is intended to correct the impression of some of the uninitiated that cryptography is some sort of occult science, possibly concerned with the study of prehistoric tombs; and the impression of others that cryptanalysis is a game somewhat like crossword puzzles, to relieve the tedium of railway journeys. Here incidents are cited to show the part that cryptography has played in diplomacy, war, literature, and — regrettably — crime. For more extensive reading in the history of the subject, the reader is referred to the Bibliography, as he is for the detailed study of individual cipher systems.

In later chapters, the fundamental principles of transposition and substitution ciphers are presented, with detailed accounts of their most important offshoots. If these are understood, any of the hundreds of ramifications and variations that stem from them will be easy to grasp. If they stand gauntly, like deciduous trees in January, they may for that reason offer a better opportunity to become familiar with their trunks, boughs, and bark; the reader can afterwards study at leisure the endless variety of foliage.

PREFACE

The section on the breaking of ciphers leads directly to the problems, which give the reader not only a practical application of his study, but also an opportunity to evaluate his skill.

The author wishes to acknowledge his indebtedness not only to the books listed in the Bibliography, but to many others, from the Middle Ages to the present day. Those cited are in his opinion the most profitable reading in their respective fields.

In particular he wants to thank Commander Lowell Cooper, U.S.N., for his careful checking of the manuscript; and Mr. Harold A. Mallice, of the New York Public Library, for his many kindnesses.

L. D. S.

*Hillsdale, New York*

# I

## *Secret Weapon Number One*

At the outbreak of the Second World War, possibly no shortage was more acute — or less publicized — than that of qualified cryptographers. Our military and naval forces are now spread over the two hemispheres. The secrecy of communications is vital. A cipher message speedily broken by the enemy may mean a major disaster for our forces.

Yet the importance of the part played by cryptographers in military operations was demonstrated to us realistically in the First World War. One instructive incident occurred in September 1918, on the eve of the great offensive against Saint-Mihiel. A student cryptographer, fresh from Washington, arrived at United States Headquarters at the front. Promptly he threw the General Staff into a state of alarm by deciphering with comparative ease a secret radio message intercepted in the American sector.

The smashing of the German salient at Saint-Mihiel was one of the most gigantic tasks undertaken by the American forces during the war. For years that salient had stabbed into the Allied lines, cutting important railways and communication lines. Its lines of defense were thought to be virtually impregnable. But for several months the Americans had been making secret preparations for attacking it and wiping it out. The stage was set, the minutest details of strategy had been determined — when the young officer of the United States Military Intelligence spread consternation through our General Staff.

The dismay at Headquarters was not caused by any new information about the strength of the enemy forces, but by the realization that the Germans must know as much about our secret plans as we did ourselves — even the exact hour set for the attack. The 'intercepted' message had been from our own base. German cryptographers were as expert as any in the world, and what had been done by an American student cryptographer could surely be done by German specialists.

The revelation was even more bitter because the cipher the young officer had broken, without any knowledge of the system, was considered absolutely safe and had long been used for most important and secret communications.[1]

From the role played by cryptography in the drama of Saint-Mihiel, one can guess what its importance was in the Second World War, when our cipher experts had to cope with Japanese and with countless other languages.

Nor is Japanese the sole challenge to our cryptanalysts. The number of languages used by the nations involved in the present war is staggering. In India alone there are 586 distinct dialects. To these must be added all the languages of the Pacific Islands, the Chinese dialects, Russian, and the languages of the Middle East and of Africa. And it is a major necessity not only to send messages secretly, and to intercept and read enemy dispatches, but also to detect information being sent out on short wave from enemy agents within our own boundaries.

The breaking of most modern cipher systems depends upon the knowledge of the letter frequencies of the language in which the message is enciphered. There are differences in the letter frequencies even of European languages. For instance, the vowel percentage of English is 40, while that of Italian and Portuguese is 48. But the difference between English letter

[1] The details of this episode are given by Herbert O. Yardley, of the U. S. Cryptographic Bureau during the First World War, in *The American Black Chamber*, Indianapolis, 1931.

frequencies and those of languages outside the Indo-European family is tremendous. In Hawaiian, for example, whose 12-letter alphabet is divided equally between vowels and consonants, the preponderance of vowels over consonants in actual word structure is enormous.[1]

In the Japanese language, however, the cryptanalysts of our armed forces encounter the most difficult problems of all. In it, complexities develop in geometric progression. Written Japanese, as differentiated from the spoken language, is based on ideographs or characters borrowed from Chinese. There are many thousands of these characters, but even moderately well-educated Japanese are rarely able to read or write more than seven or eight thousand. The Tokyo newspapers stock about 8,000 characters in each of the more frequently used sizes. Unwittingly they have furnished us with a table of ideograph frequencies, for the Tokyo Tsukiui Type Foundry has made a selection of the 5,000 most common characters, weighting them for use in magazines and newspapers. Each character is weighted according to its frequency in use.[2]

While such a frequency table might be serviceable to some extent in breaking a Japanese code, it is of no use at all in breaking a Japanese cipher.[3] Fortunately the Japanese are obliged in telegraphic enciphering to use the Morse or *kana* code. Whereas in written Japanese the true structures of declined words are not revealed, they manifest themselves immediately when the writing is romanized. And in consequence our cryptanalysts are able to break ciphers written in what is possibly the most difficult of all languages.

Our cryptographers are concerned not only with breaking

[1] The letters of the Hawaiian alphabet are *a, u, i, o, e, w* (used as a vowel); *h, k, l, m, n, p*.

[2] *A Beginners' Dictionary of Chinese-Japanese Characters*, compiled by Arthur Rose-Innes, Harvard University Press, 1942.

[3] For further discussion of the intricacies of the Japanese language, see Appendix A.

the secrecy of enemy communications. They are as much concerned with the security of our own messages. And when speed and — in order to avoid errors — simplicity are essential, the ingenuity of the encipherer is often an important factor.

One of the first instructions to those in our communications divisions is to avoid stereotyped language in secret messages. In military organizations, as in businesses and professions, there is a tendency to use standardized expressions: "In reply to yours of March 22," "Yours of January 15 at hand," "Enclosed please find." The language of commerce abounds in such stock phrases. In peacetime communications of the armed services, similar standard expressions have become traditional: "*San Francisco* departed New York for Cristobal Canal Zone. Expected time of arrival 1500 26 June." The avoidance of such conventional expressions is essential to the security of a cipher. Recently an enemy cipher was broken in a matter of minutes because, as suspected, the intercepted message began with the equivalent of "Yours."

In Army and Navy communications many words can be avoided only with great difficulty. Often it seems impossible to drop them completely. If a wholesale coffee buyer in Brazil cables to his home office in Philadelphia, it is inevitable that sooner or later he will use the word COFFEE. But if an airplane carrier must report that twenty-four planes have taken off at night, the cipher clerk has to devise ways to avoid both the words AIRPLANE and NIGHT, knowing that the enemy will be looking for them in the text. Never say the military man is without imagination. The plain-text message he transcribes may be as fantastic as "Four and twenty black birds flew out of our pie into stygian blackness." And it will be quite comprehensible to the intended receiver.

Yet in spite of all precautions, serious blunders appear to be inevitable. A mishap during World War II will illustrate. During operations a unit of one of our armed forces was in minor trouble and sent a cipher message to the report center. A half an hour later the message center received the identical message in plain text. Probably the radio operator had been handed both the enciphered message and the plain-text copy and had sent both, not realizing that they were the same. In any case, the enemy had been given the complete key to the cipher that was then in use. It was only a matter of seconds before headquarters substituted a completely different cipher and all concerned were so informed. Fortunately, because of this quick action, the enemy gained no advantage.

# II

## *The History of Secret Writing*

Cryptography (from Greek *κρυπτός, hidden,* + *γραφία, writing*) in one form or another has probably been practiced ever since man has communicated his thoughts in speech or writing. References are made to it in the Bible. One of the oldest known examples is the Spartan scytale: Plutarch tells how Lacedæmonian generals exchanged messages by winding narrow ribbons of parchment spirally around a cylindrical staff. The message was then inscribed on the parchment. When the ribbon was unwound, the writing could be read only by the person who had a cylinder of exactly the same size, upon which to rewind it, so that the letters would reappear in their normal order.[1]

Another ancient, if somewhat ludicrous, means of sending secret messages was devised by an ingenious Histiæus, when he was at the Persian court. He wished to send word to Aristagoras, his son-in-law who was in Greece, to revolt. It was, of course, vital that the message should not be intercepted. To assure secrecy Histiæus shaved the head of his most trusted slave, tattooed it with his message, and waited until the hair grew. The slave was instructed to say to Aristagoras, "Shave my head and look thereon." Aristagoras revolted. Although the speed with which communication is now possible makes this method of the fifth century B.C. appear somewhat inefficient, even during the First World War it was the practice to

[1] For the cryptanalysis of scytale communications, see pp. 92–3.

send spies across the enemy lines with messages written on their skins with invisible ink.

More scientific cryptograms were devised by the early Greeks, who frequently used arithmetical figures. One of their methods of substituting mathematical figures for letters was to block the alphabet into a square, as shown below, and to number each vertical and horizontal row from one to five. As one letter of a 26-letter alphabet must be omitted, I, in our alphabet, can be made to serve both as I and J, or U as both U and V.

| | 1 | 2 | 3 | 4 | 5 |
|---|---|---|---|---|---|
| 1 | A | F | L | Q | V |
| 2 | B | G | M | R | W |
| 3 | C | H | N | S | X |
| 4 | D | I | O | T | Y |
| 5 | E | K | P | U | Z |

Each letter of the message is indicated by the numbers of the intersecting rows, reading first the numbers from the vertical column. C becomes 31, the intersection of horizontal row 3 and vertical column 1; H is 32; and so on. To illustrate, perhaps the

22-24-51-51-52-34
32-11-41
11
33-11-23-51
12-43-24
42-44

The scytale described by Plutarch, to which we referred above, was a little more complicated than this numerical alphabet, because it disarranged the order of the letters. This shuffling of the letters to make the message unreadable is known as transposition encipherment. It is one of the two basic principles of modern cryptography. It differs fundamentally from the method employed in the square above, in that concealment is reached by disarranging the letter sequence, not by using numbers in place of the customary alphabet. This replacement of the normal letters by symbols, numbers, or other letters is the second basic principle of present-day systems, known as substitution encipherment.

The substitution of one letter for another according to a prearranged method was a favorite device of the Romans. Suetonius, in his biography of Julius Caesar, described the latter's method of secret writing. Like many of the great generals of history, Caesar seems to have been sadly lacking in cryptographic subtlety. Instead of the required letter he wrote the third letter after it — D for A, E for B, and so forth — a system which even a novice in deciphering would probably break in ten minutes. Thereafter the messages could be read almost as easily as if they were written in plain text.

Historically, one of the most interesting substitution ciphers during the Middle Ages was that of Charlemagne. He used a complete set of alphabetical equivalents that must have caused his generals many a sleepless night trying to memorize them. He had a number of different alphabets; in one of these, for example, the following character is typical.[1]

*l* = X

Perhaps the method most commonly practiced before the Renaissance was the improvised alphabet on page 19. It was a favorite among the Freemasons as late as the sixteenth century and is probably quite as popular among school children today:

[1] This is one of the most simple and consistent substitution characters used by Charlemagne. Other more esoteric symbols he used are:

*a b c d e f g h i k l m n o p q r ſ t u x y z*

| A | B | C |
|---|---|---|
| D | E | F |
| G | H | I |

J
K L
M

| N | O | P |
|---|---|---|
| Q | R | S |
| T | U | V |

W
X Y
Z

This type of cipher, or one of its variations, is frequently used by boys, with a dogged belief in the sanctity of confidential communications, and it still appears to be proof against the inquisitive eye of the teacher. Should she intercept the message below, in its grapevine transit of the schoolroom, she would think it was a meaningless scribble, and toss the priceless and soul-stirring message contemptuously into the wastepaper basket.

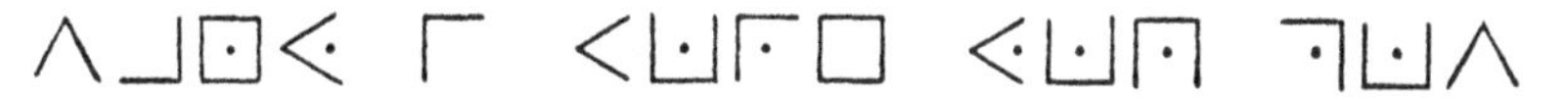

Many ingenious variations of this type of cipher were in vogue during the fifteenth century. They are generally spoken of as diagrammatic ciphers. Even in modern times such a system is easily masked in pictures, sheet music, maps, and photographs. Military censors have learned to be suspicious of even the most innocent-looking sketches or pictorial greeting cards. Although in appearance such ciphers do not resemble substitution ciphers, they are in fact nothing more than a very simple type of that system, and can be broken very easily, provided the messages are long enough, by the study of letter frequency. No matter what the substitution is, whether it is a different letter, the position of a dot, or the length of a line, the recurrence of any of these inevitably gives away the secret that at first glance seems so effectively concealed. This will be more apparent after the chapter on cryptanalysis has been read. By comparing the four cryptograms given on the following page the reader will see that the only essential difference between them is their appearance.

In each case, read from left to right, starting with the highest dot, end of line, change of direction or angle, as the case may be, and continue downwards. Each dot or stop indicates the proper letter in the alphabetical key retained by both correspondents.[1] Thus the message reads

QU IT ET RU E

The same message is given in each variation to make the identity of the four systems more obvious.

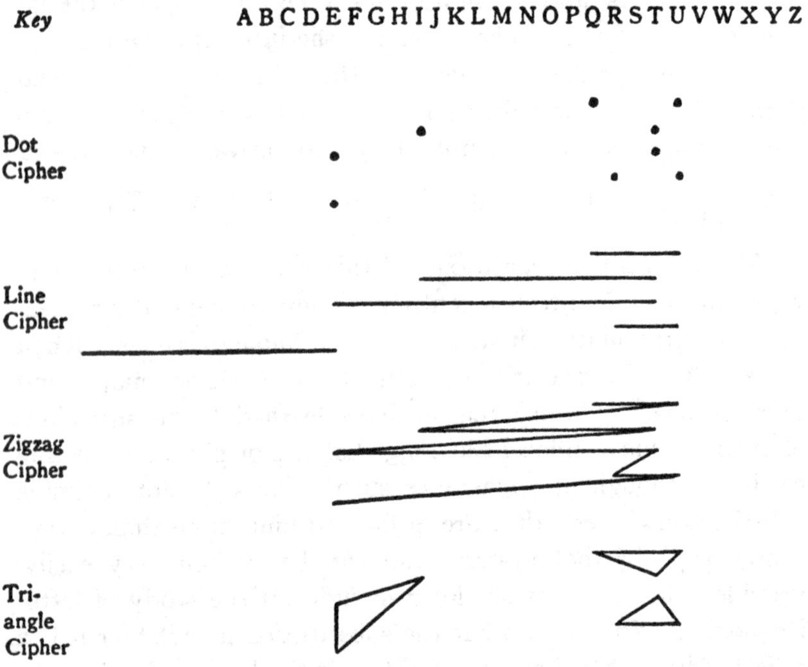

*Key* ABCDEFGHIJKLMNOPQRSTUVWXYZ

Dot Cipher

Line Cipher

Zigzag Cipher

Tri-angle Cipher

The zigzag cipher offers possibilities of further concealment. Instead of a line, a thread may be drawn from A to Z, and a small mark made on the thread to indicate the location of the first letter of the message. Then drawing the thread back from Z to A, the second letter is indicated, and the process continued

[1] In this example it is not necessary for the sender or the receiver to have an artificial key in his possession, because the spacing may be that of the standard typewriter, with the sheet inserted against the left guide.

until the entire message is enciphered. If one end of an entire spool of thread were used, and the spool then rewound by machinery, a spy might get such a message past even the most alert Intelligence organization.

Considerable interest and adeptness in cryptography were developed during the sixteenth, seventeenth, and eighteenth centuries. It was the custom in those days for people of importance to have private ciphers. The personal ciphers of Mary Stuart, the Charleses I and II, the Georges, and other English monarchs are in the possession of the British Museum and British Foreign Office. For the most part they were based on substitution, either with letters or phonetic symbols, and were nearly always so complicated that the key could not be memorized but had to be reduced to writing. In this respect they had a disadvantage inherent in codes — both correspondents had to have copies of the key.

Francis Bacon was devoted to cryptography. One of the Shakespeare-Bacon arguments is concerned with the significance of the word *honorificabilitudinitatibus*, that appears in *Love's Labour's Lost* (V, i). It is the basis for Donnelly's *The Great Cryptogram* and Mrs. Gallup's *Bi-Literal Cipher*. Probably the only unconscious humor from the pen of Mark Twain is in his treatises on the Baconian theory.

Bacon classified cryptography (which he called "cyphers") under grammar. An early admirer of his writes that Bacon's system was "one of the most ingenious methods of writing in cipher, and the most difficult to be deciphered, of any yet contrived." Possibly Bacon had his tongue in his cheek when he declared that a perfect cipher was one "not laborious to write and read." It is difficult to conceive of any more laborious to write than his biliteral cipher,[1] which had to be printed by letter press in two different type faces, the difference between them being scarcely discernible; once enciphered, the message

[1] See Appendix B.

could be deciphered only by the most complicated process, that strained not only the patience but also the eyes.

One of the most celebrated cryptanalysts, whose name, however, has come down to us as a mathematician rather than as a cipher expert, was François Viète (1540–1603). Near the end of the sixteenth century the Spanish empire extended over a considerable part of the world, and its agents were communicating with one another by means of a cipher of over 500 signs, which they varied from time to time. Some of the Spanish dispatches fell into the hands of Henry IV of France. He turned them over to Viète, who succeeded in deciphering them and was able to follow the successive variations. Henry kept this knowledge secret for two years, but then the Spaniards learned that their cipher had been broken. With righteous indignation they demanded that the Holy See have Viète tried before a Roman court as a wizard and necromancer in league with the devil. Fortunately, the Pope had a sense of the absurd and was able to share in the amusement caused by this proceeding. Although the examination was begun by a commission of cardinals, it is to this day unfinished, and the chances of an early decision seem remote.

The story of the development of military cryptography through the eighteenth, nineteenth, and twentieth centuries would fill volumes. The effects of secret writings upon the outcome of the wars and diplomatic encounters of history are innumerable, and the devices used have ranged from the writing of hidden messages in a musical score to the arrangement of the fifty-two cards in a pack so that their order carried information.

However, the employment of cryptography has not been confined to the purposes of diplomacy and warfare. It has been widely used for the sake of economy, as indicated by the numerous existing commercial codes. It has also identified itself in many ways with literature, and has even proved its value to kidnapers, gangsters, and other modern racketeers.

Even before the invention of telegraphy the possibilities of cryptography as a means of reducing postage charges occurred to people with sharp wits and small purses. Years ago in England the postage charge for carrying a letter was one shilling or more for each hundred miles. Old newspapers, however, traveled gratis, by virtue of their stamps. To the shrewd mind of the poor man this presented an opportunity. Hundreds of impecunious people stretched their budgets by placing dots over the printed letters in the journals, thus writing letters, which the government delivered without charge to the addressee.

In literature, cryptography has been the basis of the plot of such well-known stories as Maurice Leblanc's *The Hollow Needle*, Poe's *The Gold Bug*, and Jules Verne's *La Jangada.* Francis Bacon, as we have noted, was zealously interested in the art of secret writing, as was the Earl of Clarendon; and one of the world's classics, the Diary of Samuel Pepys, was written in cipher.

Whether or not, years later, the Russian Nihilists ever heard of Bacon's definition of the perfect cipher, they certainly followed his precepts. The letter given below is based on a system of secret writing commonly used by the Nihilists.

*Arnold dear, it was good news to hear that*
*you have found a job in Paris. Anna hopes*
*you will soon be able to send for her. She's*
*very eager to join you now the children are*
*both well. Sonia*

This apparently innocent letter would probably be passed over by the most painstaking censor. Yet it contains a murderous message.

The principle of this type of cryptogram is to take advantage of the peculiarity of handwriting in which all the letters of a word are not joined. The breaks are caused by the lifting of the pen, and often occur in the penmanship of people who have infrequent occasion to write. It will be observed in the note above that the endings of some of the unconnected letters point downwards while others curve upwards. The latter, whether they are the final ending of a word or not, indicate the end of the cipher group. Counting them from left to right, the decipherer takes the number in each group and pairs them, as follows:

ARN — 3, OLD — 3 (33)
DEARI — 5, T — 1 (51)
WASGO — 5, O — 1 (51)

and so on. The numerical message finally reads: 33, 51, 51, 41, 23, 43, 33, 51, 45, 12, 43, 24, 11, 34, 34, 11, 34, 34, 42, 33, 11, 44, 42, 43, 33. The numerical cipher is based on a blocked alphabet such as the Greeks used centuries ago, already described on page 17. By reference to it, it will be seen that 33 = N, 51 = E, 51 = E, 41 = D, and so on.[1]

Cryptography has long been used as a method of communicating secretly with prisoners. In England, during the days of Cromwell, Sir John Trevanion, a cavalier of distinction, having fallen from grace was locked up in Colcester Castle. He had every reason to believe that he would be put to death just as had been his friends and fellow Royalists, Sir Charles Lucas and Sir George Lisle. While awaiting his doom, however, he was one day handed the following letter by his jailer.

> Worthie Sir John: — Hope, that is ye beste comfort of ye afflicted, cannot much, I fear me, help you now. That I would saye to you, is this only: if ever I may be able to requite that I do owe you, stand not upon asking me. 'Tis not much that I can do: but what I can do, bee ye verie sure I wille. I knowe that, if dethe comes, if ordinary men fear it, it frights not you,

[1] The message finally reads: "Need money for assassination."

accounting it for a high honour, to have such a rewarde of your loyalty. Pray yet that you may be spared this soe bitter, cup. I fear not that you will grudge any sufferings; only if bie submission you can turn them away, 'tis the part of a wise man. Tell me, an if you can, to do for you anythinge that you wolde have done. The general goes back on Wednesday. Restinge your servant to command. — R. T.

If you do what Sir John did — that is, read the third letter after every punctuation mark — you may not feel the same degree of relief, but you will know that the

PANEL AT EAST END OF CHAPEL SLIDES

The prisoner asked to be allowed to pass an hour in private repentance in the chapel. But apparently being less devout than his jailers believed, he spent the hour not in prayer, but in flight.

Less fortunate and perhaps less quick-witted than Sir John was the Chevalier de Rohan, who was incarcerated in the Bastille in 1674. His accomplice in the crime for which he was imprisoned had died without confessing. De Rohan's friends realized the importance of getting this news to the prisoner secretly. If the Chevalier continued to protest his innocence, his acquittal seemed almost certain.

On the evening before his examination, de Rohan received a fresh shirt sent him from outside the prison. On one sleeve he discovered these letters:

MG DULHXCCLGU GHJ YXUJ LM CT ULGC ALJ

The Chevalier was up at the first dim light of dawn trying to decipher the meaning. Failing to do so, he confessed and paid with his life — because he could not decipher the message, which was enciphered by a simple method of substitution, L being represented by M, E by G, and so on:

LE PRISONNIER EST MORT; IL N'A RIEN DIT.

Modern criminals, as well as those of previous centuries, have recognized the advantages of cipher communication. During the years of prohibition, ships loaded with liquor communicated with bootlegging associates ashore by means of cryptographic wireless messages, in order to outwit the police and the Department of Justice.

André Langie, one of the outstanding cryptanalysts of our time, describes in his exceedingly interesting book on secret writing the case of Pastoure, a notorious bank robber. The Chief of the French Secret Service Department gave M. Langie the details of a theft from the Continental Bank. Pastoure, the thief, was not caught until six days after the robbery, and had in the interim hidden the money. Having been sentenced to five years in prison, he demanded permission to write his will almost immediately upon entering the jail. One of the pages of this document contained 144 figures closely written together. This aroused suspicion, and the paper was turned over to M. Langie for decipherment. This expert was able to arrange the digits in their proper cipher groups and then perceived that their letter frequency did not follow that of the French language, as might be expected, but of Latin.

The final decipherment read:

CALVISIUS OPUS CHRONOLOGICUM
BIBLIOTHEQUE MUNICIPALE

The prisoner had made this memorandum, apparently not trusting his memory over a period of years. He showed his wisdom in choosing an ancient manual of chronology, which could be counted on to remain indefinitely on the shelf, undisturbed. The book was a quarto tome, bound in thick leather, and under this cover M. Langie found a small thin key.

"Picture the astonishment," he writes, "then joy, of the Chief! He made me describe point by point the development of my discovery. Then he started on the chase, accompanied by his sleuth hounds. Two days later, on opening my newspaper, I learned that the thirteen hundred thousand francs which had been stolen had been recovered from the strong-room of a bank, where a compartment had been rented for fifteen years by a client about to start to South America!" [1]

In the voluminous writings on cryptography there is much disagreement about the possibility of devising a method of secret writing that would be indecipherable without a key. Many who know the amazing accomplishments of expert cryptanalysts believe it to be impossible. Such apparent miracles have been performed that not a few people are apt to conclude, as did the Spaniards of the Renaissance, that these magicians are in league with the devil. Others declare that what human cunning can reveal, it can conceal. But this is true only within certain limitations, and one of these is the necessity of being practical.

When, as in wartime, it is vitally important to transmit information secretly, it is generally equally important to communicate it speedily. Whatever opportunities television may eventually present to the cryptographer, secret communications that are to be sent by wire or radio at present must be transmitted only in letters and numerals. Reasonably quick encipherment and decipherment are obvious requirements of any cipher system. The more complicated the system, the greater the delay and the risk of error in enciphering, transmitting, and deciphering, so that complexity beyond a definite limit defeats the very end in view.

The simple expedient of using a dictionary as a code book might provide a method of secret communication that could not be broken. The number of the page and of the word on the page can easily be transmitted. But while this method is theoretically proof against detection, once a person becomes suspect and is known to be receiving code messages, his books are under suspicion too. Moreover, it is a matter of history

[1] André Langie, *Cryptographie*, Payot et Cie., Paris, 1919.

that after a sufficiently large number of messages have been intercepted, even the most cleverly devised codes have been broken.

But codes do not come within the scope of this book. They are mentioned later, briefly, only to show their difference from cryptograms. And since they, too, have been unable to cloud the eye of the professional cryptanalyst, we can perhaps be pardoned for evading a direct answer to the question of the perfect secret writing, thus emulating the age-old wisdom of the Sphinx.

Even in cryptography, silence is golden.

# III

## *Transposition Ciphers*

The majority of the cipher variations described or suggested in the preceding pages have little practical interest for the secret agents of our army or navy, for whom cryptography is a necessary and vital means of daily communication. Their cipher systems can take any form or shape, or move along the most devious route, but it must be methodical, and of a type to be written and read with reasonable speed. It need not insure permanent security, but only sufficient security to resist efforts at breaking it until the objectives of the correspondents have been reached.

As we stated earlier, all ciphers are based upon two fundamental principles, transposition and substitution. There is no other possibility except that of combining the two methods. This seeming simplicity, however, should cause no overconfidence in the student. The ease that it suggests will be discovered all too soon to be but a mirage.

Transposition ciphers are formed by changing the normal position of the units that make up the message in plain language. These units are usually individual letters. A common game played by children illustrates one method of altering the familiar order. It is to write the entire message backwards, or to write the letters of each word of the message in that way.

Cipher text:

EHT DLIHC SI REHTAF OT EHT NAM

Clear text:

THE CHILD IS FATHER TO THE MAN

This juvenile trick for obscuring a message serves quite as well as a complex cipher to illustrate the principle of all transposition, namely, that units are altered in relative position only, and that they retain their original identity, A remaining A; B, B; and so on. This is, in brief, the essence of the transposition method.

Anagrams present another familiar example of this type of transposition. In this game the letters of words are regrouped to form new words. The original sequence EAR is changed to ARE or ERA; DEAR to READ or DARE. Skill of this kind is the test of merit. For example, the solution of the anagram LOVE TO RUIN is REVOLUTION.

In the seventeenth century anagrams were an admired accomplishment and a favorite diversion for the poets. The MARY–ARMYgram of George Herbert, which appears in one of his popular poems, is not the least diverting of its kind:

MARY

ANA GRAM

ARMY

*How well her name an* ARMY *doth present,*
*In whom the Lord of Hosts did pitch His tent!*

More ingenious still, and quite as much in vogue during the same period, were palindromes — words, verses, or sentences that read the same forward as backward. Examples are:

REPAPER
NAME NO ONE MAN
MADAM, I'M ADAM
ABLE WAS I ERE I SAW ELBA

Acrostics fall into the same class. In these the initial, middle, or last letters of each line, taken consecutively, form words. The intent, of course, is to form a cipher which the writer may or may not wish to have discovered. It is sometimes possible to find acrostics even where they were never intended to be, as any opponent of the Baconian theory of Shakespeare's writings will insist.

Acrostics can be very complex: single, double, or triple. Whereas they often are intricate, embodied in a prose passage or a poem, a list of words will serve as a simple example to illustrate the fundamental principle:

MinueT
UnanimouS
StratA
IncertitudE
CreatoR
HubbuB
AppreciatE
TranslatinG
HemiplegiA
ChekhoV
HarmonicA
AristophaneS
RetinuE
MackintosH
SoliciT
TrianglE
OverflourisH
SobriqueT
OctavO

If all the initial letters are read downwards, and all the final letters upwards, the acrostic appears.

Transposition ciphers are to some extent analogous to jigsaw puzzles. In such puzzles and ciphers, if all the pieces are present and in proper order, a clear picture of the message exists. If they are mixed up, all of the elements are still present, but have no apparent meaning. If the disorder is brought about by random shuffling, only long and painstaking attempts by trial and error can bring them back to normal order. Since practical cryptography is not a puzzle aiming to test the patience, but is the science of secret communication, its object is to arrange some sort of systematic disorder, which can be set right quickly and accurately by the one for whom the secret message is intended.

The absolute necessity for system becomes apparent when one realizes the variety of arrangement made possible by transposing letters. The following table shows how quickly the combinations run into figures that one is accustomed to apply only when discussing the war appropriations. It represents the possible variations in groups of from three to twenty letters:

| | |
|---|---|
| 3 letters | 6 |
| (*for example*, THE, TEH, HET, HTE, ETH, EHT) | |
| 4 letters | 24 |
| 5 letters | 120 |
| 6 letters | 720 |
| 7 letters | 5,040 |
| 8 letters | 40,320 |
| 9 letters | 362,880 |
| 10 letters | 3,628,800 |
| 11 letters | 39,916,800 |
| 12 letters | 479,001,600 |
| 13 letters | 6,227,020,800 |
| 14 letters | 87,178,291,200 |
| 15 letters | 1,307,674,368,000 |
| 16 letters | 20,922,789,880,000 |
| 17 letters | 355,687,427,960,000 |
| 18 letters | 6,402,373,703,280,000 |
| 19 letters | 121,645,100,362,320,000 |
| 20 letters | 2,432,902,007,246,400,000[1] |

Obviously trial-and-error methods are out of the question for deciphering a message in any language — modern, ancient, do-

[1] "The information given above has been obtained from sources we believe are reliable. We are not responsible for errors or omissions."

mestic, or foreign — if the message is made up of a sequence of symbols like the alphabet.

There are two practical methods, however, by which the letters of a message may be scrambled and subsequently reduced to order again. These can be stated simply enough, no matter how difficult the execution frequently proves to be. They are: (1) the use of geometrical forms or patterns to aid both the enciphering and deciphering; and (2) the establishment of a procedure for disarranging of letters by taking a specific route to inscribe the plain text within the chosen pattern, and following another definite route for transcribing the cipher text. This method is known as transposition. These two methods will be dealt with in order.

## Geometrical Patterns

The restrictions of practical cryptography demand that the pattern used must take the form of a relatively simple geometrical figure, not only because the possibility of error is increased in proportion to the complexity of the pattern, but also because the necessity for haste in deciphering is frequently vital. Even when speed is not an important consideration, the constitutional carelessness of mankind has a fourfold opportunity to express itself. The two operations (inscription and transcription) have to be performed by two people, the sender and the receiver. The possibility of error becomes a matter of considerable importance unless the key is reduced to writing — a perilous practice at best. Once an enemy agent is suspected of having a key in his possession he is in grave peril as long as he retains it.

Abandoning, then, for the moment, schemes that require memoranda, we shall consider first geometrical figures that require no written record, beginning with those that place no undue tax on the rare faculty of good memory.

One comparatively simple use of geometrical figures is employed in what is called vertical writing. For example, the message A LITTLE KNOWLEDGE is written in two vertical columns, as shown below (geometrical figure $2 \times 8$):

```
A N
L O
I W
T L
T E
L D
E G
K E
```

The cipher text is then taken from the horizontal pairs thus formed, so that the message becomes:

AN LO IW TL TE LD EG KE

It may now be divided into groups of four letters to read,

ANLO IWTL TELD EGKE

Four-letter group lengths are suggested here because the message contains sixteen letters, a number equally divisible by four. The group lengths for cipher messages, however, are quite arbitrary, or depend on the individual cipher. The important thing is that the cipher be divided into groups of regular lengths, whatever they may be, because regular division brings about an artificial break and disguises the normal word division of the plain text.

The most common group length for ciphers is one of five letters. The practical reason for this is the widespread use of the telegraph in civil, diplomatic, or military cryptography. For the sake of speed and accuracy over the wires, it is important to transmit in groups of equal length, as the five-letter interval is less susceptible to error by both sender and receiver.

The message given above could also be written horizontally instead of vertically. In that event it would appear thus:

A L I T T L E K
N O W L E D G E

The cipher message is taken from the vertical pairs with the same result as before:

ANLO IWTL TELD EGKE

The geometrical figures formed by these two mechanical methods are rectangles formed in this way:

```
A N     A L I T T L E K
L O     N O W L E D G E
I W
T L
T E
L D
E G
K E
```

The only other geometrical figure that can encompass a sixteen-letter text is a square:

```
A L I T
T L E K
N O W L
E D G E
```

The uses of practical cryptography restrict the choice of design to figures that are essentially simple, such as the triangle, the square, the rectangle, or the trapezoid. The elaborate frames often employed in fictional cryptography are so easily subject to error that they would be inevitably avoided by an experienced agent.

Practicality places restrictions on transposition enciphering, not only in the shape of the design, but also in its size. At first thought it might seem as if the larger the figure used, the greater would be the concealment. This is not true. The fallacy has been understood since the time of Copernicus. One can travel only so far without returning to the starting place.

The geometrical figures formed by a message of seventy-two letters offer about the practical maximum of opportunity, since they afford ten different patterns. As will be shown, an increase in size does not necessarily provide greater possibilities for combination.

The rectangular patterns afforded by seventy-two units are: 2 × 36, 3 × 24, 4 × 18, 6 × 12, 8 × 9, 9 × 8, 12 × 6, 18 × 4, 24 × 3, and 36 × 2 — ten in all. To increase the size to ninety-six, on the other hand, would still give only ten possibilities: 2 × 48, 3 × 32, 4 × 24, 6 × 16, 8 × 12, 12 × 8, 16 × 6, 24 × 4, 32 × 3, and 48 × 2. By increasing to one hundred, we should have: 2 × 50, 4 × 25, 5 × 20, 10 × 10, 20 × 5, 25 × 4, and 50 × 2 — a decrease to seven patterns.

The table on page 37 will serve as a visual aid. The message is:

*A lock obtained with guilt and kept with pain,*
*Is sought in every place, and sought in vain.*

It will be noticed that the slightly misquoted seventy-two word message borrowed from Pope has been inscribed in all the possible rectangles. For purposes of concealment, the transcription of the letters is made in the direction which is at right angles to the direction of the inscription. Thus the 36 × 2 pattern is transcribed as follows:

AOKBANDIHULADETIHANSOGTNVRPAENSUHIVI
LCOTIEWTGITNKPWTPIISUHIEEYLCADOGTNAN

and may be grouped into six-letter units for convenience:

AOKBAN DIHULA DETIHA NSOGTN VRPAEN SUHIVI
LCOTIE WTGITN KPWTPI ISUHIE EYLCAD OGTNAN

Similarly, the 6 × 12 pattern is transcribed:

ADDNVSLWKIEOOIESRUCTPSYG
KHTOPHOGWULTBUIGAITITHCN
ALHTEVITPIAANAANNIENIEDN

36 × 2

A O K B A N D I H U L A D E T I H A N S O G T N V R P A E N S U H I V I
L C O T I E W T G I T N K P W T P I I S U H I E E Y L C A D O G T N A N

2 × 36

A N
L I
O S
C S
K O
O U
B G
T H
A T
I I
N N
E E
D V
W E
I R
T Y
H P
G L
U A
I C
L E
T A
A N
N D
D S
K O
E U
P G
T H
W T
I I
T N
H V
P A
A I
I N

24 × 3

A C B I D T U T D P I P N S G I V Y A A S G I A
L K T N W H I A K T T A I O H N E P C N O H N I
O O A E I G L N E W H I S U T E R L E D U T V N

3 × 24

A D V
L K E
O E R
C P Y
K T P
O W L
B I A
T T C
A H E
I P A
N A N
E I D
D N S
W I O
I S U
T S G
H O H
G U T
U G I
I H N
L T V
T I A
A N I
N E N

18 × 4

A K A D H L D T H N O T V P E S H V
L O I W G T K W P I U I E L A O T A
O B N I U A E I A S G N R A N U I I
C T E T I N P T I S H E Y C D G N N

4 × 18

A U N A
L I I C
O L S E
C T S A
K A O N
O N U D
B D G S
T K H O
A E T U
I P I G
N T N H
E W E T
D I V I
W T E N
I H R V
T P Y A
H A P I
G I L N

8 × 9

A I U P N I A G
L N I T I N C H
O E L W S E E T
C D T I S V A I
K W A T O E N N
O I N H U R D V
B T D P G Y S A
T H K A H P O I
A G E I T L U N

9 × 8

A A H D H O V E H
L I G K P U E A T
O N U E A G R N I
C E I P I H Y D N
K D L T N T P S V
O W T W I I L O A
B I A I S N A U I
T T N T S E C G N

6 × 12

A D D N V S
L W K I E O
O I E S R U
C T P S Y G
K H T O P H
O G W U L T
B U I G A I
T I T H C N
A L H T E V
I T P I A A
N A A N N I
E N I E D N

12 × 6

A B D U D I N G V A S I
L T W I K T I H E C O N
O A I L E H S T R E U V
C I T T P P S I Y A G A
K N H A T A O N P N H I
O E G N W I U E L D T N

TABLE OF GEOMETRIC PATTERNS

and, for variety's sake, may be grouped into eight-letter units:

ADDNVSLW KIEOOIES RUCTPSYG
KHTOPHOG WULTBUIG AITITHCN
ALHTEVIT PIAANAAN NIENIEDN

Before leaving the subject of the construction of patterns for transposition encipherment, some mention should be made of devices that require written memoranda or other aids to the memory. Although these do not come within the scope of practical modern cryptography, they have played important roles in many great dramas of the past. Some have been referred to previously — for example, the Spartan scytale and the diagrammatic ciphers (see pp. 19–20) which the reader will now recognize as true transposition ciphers. Transposition need not, however, be confined to the arrangement of single letters. The order in which words are read may determine their significance.

## Grilles

One device that effectively conceals the proper reading order of words is known as a grille. It is usually made of a sheet of paper or celluloid in which holes are cut in purposeful positions. This sheet, or grille, is superimposed upon the plain message and the secret message is read through the windows of the grille.

Suppose a soldier must report secretly to his commanding officer about the imminence of war. We may suppose, in most cases, that a soldier would write some prosaic lines to cover the hidden message. It would take no less than a poet-soldier — Byron in fact — to dash off the verses at the top of page 39.

Upon receiving these verses the commanding officer places over them a grille that is a facsimile of the one Byron used.

By reading only the words that appear through the windows the poet's hidden message is revealed:

MUSTERING SQUADRON FORMING RANKS WAR NEAR

*And there was mounting in hot haste the steed,*
*The mustering squadron and the clattering car,*
*And swiftly forming in the ranks of war;*
*And deep the thunder peal on peal afar;*
*And near, the beat of the alarming drum*
*Roused up the soldier ere the morning star*
*While thronged the citizens with terror dumb*
*Or whispering, with white lips, — 'the*
*foe! they come, they come!'*

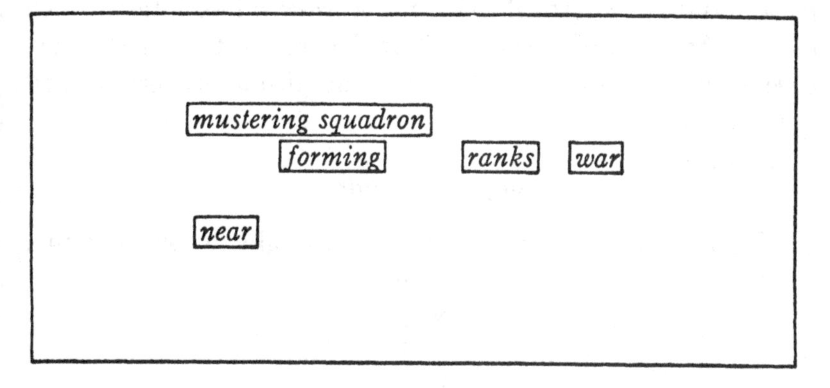


The reader can for his own account devise simple or intricate grilles that will disclose any desired information in the most familiar lines of his favorite poet. It is easy enough to construct exceptionally clever grilles; they can be given many arrangements and many variations. But they are all subject to the same weakness. They must, of necessity, be carried about, and may be lost or stolen. The amateur cryptographer or the writer of detective fiction may test his ingenuity by inventing grilles; however, the military man in the zone of action had better exert his faculties along other lines.

## Route Transcription

Returning to the geometrical designs for practical use, it will be noticed that in the designs given on page 37 the messages all were inscribed by following the same route — downwards, in succeeding vertical columns to the right. It must have already occurred to the reader that the routes can be varied almost *ad infinitum.* There are innumerable ways to bring about a "sweet disorder" in writing ciphers. The simplest variation of vertical writing is horizontal inscription, which follows the route of normal writing, left to right. For the purpose we use a shorter text, but one that adequately serves as an illustration:

Plain text:

VENI VIDI VICI

The message is inscribed from left to right in two columns:

V E
N I
V I
D I
V I
C I

Transcribing vertically and grouping into four-letter units, we obtain the cipher text:

VNVD VCEI IIII.

It should be noted that the same result is obtained with a different geometrical pattern, as shown below, provided the dimensions are the same and the message is inscribed vertically and transcribed horizontally:

V N V D V C
E I I I I I

Cipher text:

VNVD VCEI IIII

The same end is reached by what is known as *rail-fence transposition* or *zigzag writing* — the routing obtained by writing the message thus:

V N V D V C
 E I I I I I

The great variability of routes can easily be demonstrated by tracing a few of them through the geometrical pattern of 6 × 4. Those given below are chosen as suitable for practical use. Considerably more complicated routes can be plotted, of course, but they almost inevitably lead to error.

In the tables given below, in order to make the routing more easily discernible, the plain-text message used is the alphabet: ABC . . . X (Y and Z are omitted). Since it is possible for each route to have a different starting point, variations 1, 2, 3, et cetera, show the same route started from the different corners of the rectangle.

## ORTHOGONAL ROUTES

### A. *Simple Horizontal*

| 1 | 2 | 3 | 4 |
|---|---|---|---|
| A B C D E F | F E D C B A | S T U V W X | X W V U T S |
| G H I J K L | L K J I H G | M N O P Q R | R Q P O N M |
| M N O P Q R | R Q P O N M | G H I J K L | L K J I H G |
| S T U V W X | X W V U T S | A B C D E F | F E D C B A |

### B. *Simple Vertical*

| 1 | 2 | 3 | 4 |
|---|---|---|---|
| A E I M Q U | U Q M I E A | D H L P T X | X T P L H D |
| B F J N R V | V R N J F B | C G K O S W | W S O K G C |
| C G K O S W | W S O K G C | B F J N R V | V R N J F B |
| D H L P T X | X T P L H D | A E I M Q U | U Q M I E A |

### C. *Alternate Horizontal*

| 1 | 2 | 3 | 4 |
|---|---|---|---|
| ABCDEF<br>LKJIHG<br>MNOPQR<br>XWVUTS | FEDCBA<br>GHIJKL<br>RQPONM<br>STUVWX | XWVUTS<br>MNOPQR<br>LKJIHG<br>ABCDEF | STUVWX<br>RQPONM<br>GHIJKL<br>FEDCBA |

### D. *Alternate Vertical*

| 1 | 2 | 3 | 4 |
|---|---|---|---|
| AHIPQX<br>BGJORW<br>CFKNSV<br>DELMTU | XQPIHA<br>WROJGB<br>VSNKFC<br>UTMLED | DELMTU<br>CFKNSV<br>BGJORW<br>AHIPQX | UTMLED<br>VSNKFC<br>WROJGB<br>XQPIHA |

## DIAGONAL ROUTES

### E. *Simple Diagonal*

| 1 | 2 | 3 | 4 |
|---|---|---|---|
| ABDGKO<br>CEHLPS<br>FIMQTV<br>JNRUWX | OKGDBA<br>SPLHEC<br>VTQMIF<br>XWURNJ | GKOSVX<br>DHLPTW<br>BEIMQU<br>ACFJNR | XVSOKG<br>WTPLHD<br>UQMIEB<br>RNJFCA |

| 5 | 6 | 7 | 8 |
|---|---|---|---|
| ACFJNR<br>BEIMQU<br>DHLPTW<br>GKOSVX | RNJFCA<br>UQMIEB<br>WTPLHD<br>XVSOKG | JNRUWX<br>FIMQTV<br>CEHLPS<br>ABDGKO | XWURNJ<br>VTQMIF<br>SPLHEC<br>OKGDBA |

*F. Alternate Diagonal*

| 1 | 2 | 3 | 4 |
|---|---|---|---|
| A B F G N O | O N G F B A | G N O U V X | X V U O N G |
| C E H M P U | U P M H E C | F H M P T W | W T P M H F |
| D I L Q T V | V T Q L I D | B E I L Q S | S Q L I E B |
| J K R S W X | X W S R K J | A C D J K R | R K J D C A |

| 5 | 6 | 7 | 8 |
|---|---|---|---|
| A C D J K R | R K J D C A | J K R S W X | X W S R K J |
| B E I L Q S | S Q L I E B | D I L Q T V | V T Q L I D |
| F H M P T W | W T P M H F | C E H M P U | U P M H E C |
| G N O U V X | X V U O N G | A B F G N O | O N G F B A |

## SPIRAL ROUTES

*G. Clockwise*

| 1 | 2 | 3 | 4 |
|---|---|---|---|
| A B C D E F | L M N O P A | D E F G H I | I J K L M N |
| P Q R S T G | K V W X Q B | C R S T U J | H U V W X O |
| O X W V U H | J U T S R C | B Q X W V K | G T S R Q P |
| N M L K J I | I H G F E D | A P O N M L | F E D C B A |

*H. Counterclockwise*

| 1 | 2 | 3 | 4 |
|---|---|---|---|
| A P O N M L | F E D C B A | N M L K J I | I H G F E D |
| B Q X W V K | G T S R Q P | O X W V U H | J U T S R C |
| C R S T U J | H U V W X O | P Q R S T G | K V W X Q B |
| D E F G H I | I J K L M N | A B C D E F | L M N O P A |

It is apparent that instead of following normal direction of ordinary writing from left to right and from above downwards, the letters of the plain text may take the order of any of the routes shown in the tables, and afterwards be transcribed to form the cipher text by taking the letters out of the rectangle to follow the path of any other route shown.

Since all texts are not designed to fit exactly into a rectangle of 24 cells, there is a possibility that one or more cells will remain vacant. When this happens the empty cells are filled with letters having no significance but which are inserted as fillers. These are known as "nulls" or "dummies." Whether the nulls are placed at the beginning or end is immaterial, but it is necessary that they be given their position before the process of transposition is begun.

When, on the other hand, the message is slightly too long to suit the diagram, a larger rectangle may be used. If the message is very much too long the same diagram may be repeated.

For purposes of illustration, let us suppose that we are required to devise a transposition cipher. The occasion is momentous, secrecy essential.

Four details must be prearranged:

1. The size and shape of the geometrical pattern.

2. The starting place and the route by which the message will be inscribed.

3. The starting place and direction for transcription.

4. The group lengths for the final cipher text. (If the message is to be delivered in writing, it may be divided into any letter-group lengths; if it is to be delivered verbally over the telephone or radio, or transmitted by telegraph or wireless, caution suggests the established rule of five-letter lengths.)

We decide on the four points as follows:

1. To use a completely filled rectangle of six columns and four rows.

2. To inscribe the letters of the plain text within this rectangle by taking the route of B–1, shown on page 41, starting in the top left-hand corner.

3. To transcribe the thus inscribed letters by following route G–4 to form the cipher text.

4. To use four-letter groups in the cryptogram.

Suppose our message is:

ENEMY PLANS ATTACK AT DAWN

Since it contains a total of twenty-two letters, and it has been agreed to use a completely filled rectangle of twenty-four, it is necessary to add two nulls to make the pattern complete. We therefore make the rectangle and fill it in as follows:

```
E Y N T A W
N P S A T N
E L A C D G
M A T K A M
```

The italic letters *G* and *M* are nulls.

We now transcribe the message according to route G–4, which, it will be remembered, is spiral clockwise, beginning in the lower right-hand corner, and divide it into groups of four letters:

MAKT AMEN EYNT AWNG DCAL PSAT

When our colleague receives the message, he deciphers it according to the prearranged plan. To do this, the process is merely reversed. In a rectangle of six columns and four rows, he writes the message according to route G–4. The plain text letters are then taken out by the path of B–1, starting in the upper left-hand corner and following a simple vertical route.

At this point some comment should be made upon the choice of the two nulls, G and M. These were not picked at random, but were sensible selections, advisedly made. In the first place, they are letters of reasonably frequent occurrence in our language and therefore not obviously nulls. Letters of infrequent occurrence, such as J, K, Q, X, and Z, should never be used as dummies, since they are quickly recognized.

This restriction involves an important principle. Since transposition ciphers consist merely of rearrangements of letters without any change in spelling, the normal frequency of the letters used likewise remains unchanged. The letters of every alphabetical language have characteristic frequencies that afford valuable clues in cryptanalysis. The presence of letters of very low frequency, such as Q and Z, is so unusual that they are apt to be identified as nulls. (See the tables of letter frequency, pages 153–54.) Once the nulls are known, the number of letters in the plain text is easily found, and the beginning and end of the actual message; then it is much easier to discover the route that has been followed.

A second value in using common letters as nulls is that they may cause an enemy analyst to confuse a transposition cipher with a substitution encipherment. This possibility will be more apparent after the discussion of substitution ciphers in the next chapter.

Having successfully mastered a comparatively simple cipher routing, the cryptographer may now attempt a more complicated method of route transcription.

Suppose we wish to inscribe the line:

AND FOOLS WHO CAME TO SCOFF REMAINED TO PRAY

The prearranged scheme, or key, this time is:

1. To use a completely filled square of six columns.

2. To inscribe the letters of the plain text within the square by an alternate diagonal route, beginning in the lower left-hand corner, and moving from left to right (F–3).

3. To transcribe the letters by following a simple diagonal route, beginning in the upper right-hand corner, and progressing from right to left (E–6).

4. To use four-letter groups in the cipher text.

Encipherment:

```
T A I P R Y
E O M N O A
L M S E E T
O S A C R D
N O W C O F
A D F H O F
```

Cipher text:

```
YART OPDE NIFR
EMAF OCSO TOCA
MEHW SLFO ODNA
```

The reader may test his skill in deciphering by using the reverse process as described in the previous example.

The security of all ciphers discussed so far is not great, in spite of the fact that they have afforded a large degree of variability. Note, for instance, that all five letters of the word ENEMY manifest themselves in our war message, AMEN EYNT (page 45); AND can easily be picked out of the final group ODNA of the encipherment just completed. Although such defects may seem inconsequential to the amateur, they lead the professional cryptanalyst quickly to the cipher key. This inherent weakness may be to a large extent remedied, however, by columnar transposition.

## Columnar Transposition

We have observed that practicality suggests that the limits of geometric patterns for transposition ciphers are from two to twelve columns and from two to twelve rows. We add nulls and choose routes with a view toward confusing a hostile analyst; and his confusion can be greatly increased by an arbitrary disarrangement of the columns or rows. If we decide that in a pattern of four columns we shall transpose each column into another position, we are able, to a degree, to confound our enemy.

We must of course have some agreement with our colleagues on the procedure for transposition. We might agree that the receiver of a message is to arrange it in four columns of five letters each, for example. Thus he would get the message

AS IDLE AS A PAINTED SHIP

in the form:

| 1 | 2 | 3 | 4 |
|---|---|---|---|
| A | D | S | I |
| L | S | E | A |
| A | I | P | A |
| N | D | T | E |
| S | P | H | I |

He is to rearrange these columns according to our plan. We can base this plan on a memory aid, perhaps a date or other number easily recalled. The example we are now considering is based on 1492. The receiver rearranges the four figures of this date in their ascending order: 1249, then heads the message columns with them:

| 1 | 2 | 4 | 9 |
|---|---|---|---|
| 1 | 2 | 3 | 4 |
| A | D | S | I |
| L | S | E | A |
| A | I | P | A |
| N | D | T | E |
| S | P | H | I |

Next, he puts the columns into the normal order of our date key:

| 1 | 4 | 9 | 2 |
|---|---|---|---|
| 1 | 3 | 4 | 2 |
| A | S | I | D |
| L | E | A | S |
| A | P | A | I |
| N | T | E | D |
| S | H | I | P |

In short messages, the use of such memory aids is perfectly adequate, and no clue need be put on paper. However, if we are dealing with a long sequence of columns and wish to transpose them or transcribe them in a complicated order, we should put an undue tax on the memory, especially if we had to recall the sequence after an extended period of time. A convenient device to assist the memory in such circumstances is the key word. A word is chosen — preferably one in which no letter is repeated — and the position or order in which the columns are to be read is indicated alphabetically. For example, we could choose the word MACBETH. By arranging the letters in this word in their alphabetical sequence we have

| 1 | 2 | 3 | 4 | 5 | 6 | 7 |
|---|---|---|---|---|---|---|
| A | B | C | E | H | M | T |

or

| 6 | 1 | 3 | 2 | 4 | 7 | 5 |
|---|---|---|---|---|---|---|
| M | A | C | B | E | T | H. |

The word MACBETH is technically known as the key word and the number 6132475 as the derived numerical key.

One can transpose the rows of a geometric pattern by the same method, by writing the numerical key vertically instead of horizontally; or, the two procedures can be combined by the use of two key words, one to be used horizontally, and the other vertically.

The word MACBETH contains seven different letters. If we had chosen a word in which a letter is repeated, the letter would take its proper number the first time it occurs, and the next consecutive number in its next position. For example:

| 4 | 8 | 5 | 1 | 2 | 6 | 3 | 7 |
|---|---|---|---|---|---|---|---|
| M | U | R | D | E | R | E | R |

R is used three times and carries the numbers 5, 6, and 7. E occurs twice, and is numbered 2 and 3. For longer messages, this method may be extended to phrases.

Like nulls, key words should not be chosen at random, but should be selected wisely. The following points should be borne in mind in making the selection:

1. The key should be something which can be easily remembered, such as, CASEY AT THE BAT.

2. The words should admit of but one spelling. JUDGEMENT would be inadvisable because it would be poor *judgment* to select a word which has two admissible spellings.

3. The meaning should present no association with the text to which it is the key. MONEY would be a poor key for the cryptographic text, NEED FUNDS TO CONTINUE PROPAGANDA.

In columnar keyed transposition, as has been illustrated (pages 48–49), the letters are written in a geometrical design, usually a rectangle, by inscribing them in the ordinary manner of writing, from left to right and from top downwards, and then transcribing them by "reading" the columns in the order determined by the numerical key. If the message is not sufficiently long to fill the last line, nulls are used.

For the sake of variety let us now experiment with the encipherment of a line of modern verse.

Plain text:

WAS IT FOR THIS I UTTERED PRAYERS

Key word:

EDNA MILLAY

This key word is a bad choice since Miss Millay is the author — see rule 3 above. But we will use it. Then the numerical key is:

43918567210

| Normal order: | 1 | 2 | 3 | 4 | 5 | 6 | 7 | 8 | 9 | 10 |
|---|---|---|---|---|---|---|---|---|---|---|
| | W | A | S | I | T | F | O | R | T | H |
| | I | S | I | U | T | T | E | R | E | D |
| | P | R | A | Y | E | R | S | *B* | *C* | *G* |
| Numerical key: | 4 | 3 | 9 | 1 | 8 | 5 | 6 | 7 | 2 | 10 |

Note: *B*, *C*, *G*, are nulls.

The message is then transcribed according to the numerical key

IUY TEC ASR WIP FTR OES RRB TTE SIA HDG

and broken into five-letter groups for the cipher text:

IUYTE CASRW IPFTR OESRR BTTES IAHDG

To decipher this, prepare a rectangle having as many columns as the key word has letters, and as many rows as the letters of the message require. Since the key word has ten letters, and the message thirty, the rectangle drawn is $10 \times 3$. The columns are then numbered according to the numerical key (Figure 1). The cipher text is then filled in the proper

| 4 | 3 | 9 | 1 | 8 | 5 | 6 | 7 | 2 | 10 |
|---|---|---|---|---|---|---|---|---|---|
| | | | | | | | | | |
| | | | | | | | | | |
| | | | | | | | | | |

FIGURE 1

columns in groups of three (Figure 2). Not until the procedure has been completed does the clear text appear (Figure 3).

| 4 | 3 | 9 | 1 | 8 | 5 | 6 | 7 | 2 | 10 |
|---|---|---|---|---|---|---|---|---|---|
| | A | | I | | | | | T | |
| | S | | U | | | | | E | |
| | R | | Y | | | | | C | |

FIGURE 2

| 4 | 3 | 9 | 1 | 8 | 5 | 6 | 7 | 2 | 10 |
|---|---|---|---|---|---|---|---|---|---|
| W | A | S | I | T | F | O | R | T | H |
| I | S | I | U | T | T | E | R | E | D |
| P | R | A | Y | E | R | S | B | C | G |

FIGURE 3

This method of transposition has the advantage of offering considerable variation by means of changing the key word. For instance, a change can be prearranged to take effect daily, or every third day, or weekly, or even according to arithmetical or geometric progression of dates. This key series is then automatic and does not need to be inscribed in the cipher. It is also possible to prepare a long list of suitable keys, and to designate each key by an indicator which is inserted in the cryptogram in a known position. In the *Millay* cipher, given above, for example, the first null, B, might indicate the second in a prearranged list of key words. The danger in this is that if an error should occur in the part of the cipher containing the indicator, the difficulty of deciphering would be almost insurmountable. For this reason, indicators, if used, should be inserted in one of two positions — near the beginning and the end.

The degree of cipher security in columnar transposition can be greatly increased by the prearranged use of incompletely filled rectangles. An example of this method is the following text of twenty-six letters inserted in a geometric pattern of 5 × 6, or thirty cells:

Plain text:

FOR NEVER WAS A STORY OF MORE WOE

Key word:

R O M E O

Numerical key:

```
5 3 2 1 4
F O R N E
V E R W A
S A S T O
R Y O F M
O R E W O
E
```

Cipher:

NW TF WR RS OE OE AY RE AO MO FV SR OE

Any analyst into whose hands this might fall, if he did not know of the prearranged plan, would first assume that the pattern might be one of the multiples of 26, either 2 × 13, or 13 × 2. Getting nowhere with these, he must experiment with numerous other possibilities, such as a rectangle of 6 × 4, with an indicator letter added at the beginning and end. Even though he may eventually be successful — and the professional analyst usually succeeds — he will lose much time in experimentation.

The rightful receiver of the cryptogram will have no difficulty. He first prepares a rectangle of 5 × 6, and crosses out the last four cells in the bottom row, as agreed. He then inserts the cipher text in key-number order and the clear text evolves.

## Summary

The foregoing discussion includes all of the basic principles of transposition ciphers. Although, as we have remarked, the variations in application approach infinity, the basic principles remain the same no matter how ingenious the variation may be. Since this is so, the time required by the cryptanalyst to break a cipher is measured by his own ingenuity, experience, and by the element of luck.

It may be helpful to review some of the more practical variations.

*Pattern.* Although a rectangle is the most convenient shape for transposition purposes, any geometric design may be used, such as the triangle, the polygon, the trapezoid, or any other figure that is symmetrical.

*Route.* Conventional route variations have been shown (see page 41), but much more devious paths may be chosen if one wishes. In general, however, intricate routes have the disadvantage that some form of memoranda showing the route must be made and retained by both parties. For instance, a route that represents a succession of the moves of a knight in chess may be selected. Again, one may use a grille that is quite different from that described on pages 38–9. It can conveniently be made by cutting windows in a square of cross-section (graph) paper. These windows should form an irregular pattern, and be the same size as the squares of the paper. The grille so formed is then superimposed on another sheet of exactly the same size, and the first letters of the message written through the windows onto the sheet underneath. When all cells revealed by the perforations in the upper sheet have been filled, the grille is turned 90° in either direction as agreed. The new cells so revealed now receive the next letters of the message. A properly made grille can be given four 90° turns, each turn exposing new blank cells beneath the apertures for additional letters.

This method of inscription causes a very erratic disarrangement of letters composing the message. The grille is then removed and the disarranged letters may be transcribed according to any route agreed upon. Naturally both the sender and the receiver of the message must have identical grilles.

*Polyliteral transposition.* A variation may be made in the size of the unit transposed. One need not transpose single letters at a time. Pairs of letters, or groups of three, four, or five letters, may be employed in the same manner as that used in monoliteral or single-letter transposition.

*Spelling.* Since the first signs of approaching success in breaking a cipher are the appearance of common letter combinations that suggest the formation of words or syllables, words spelled phonetically and misspelled words may help to obscure the process used. For example, CONSTERNATION may be written KON STUR NEIGH SHUN. To the hostile analyst the letter sequences, KON, KONST, KONSTURN, and the like, would not be so apt to disclose the fact that he had hit upon the right track as would the appearance of such common groups as CONS, CONSTERN, and so on.

In the examples given so far, only a single transposition has been used. It is quite possible to repeat the transposing process a second time. Thus, after we have arrived at a cipher text by any of the processes already described:

Cipher text: VNVD VCEI IIII

Plain text: *VENI VIDI VICI*

we may inscribe the cipher groups again:

V N V D
V C E I
I I I I

and transcribe them by any route we wish, such as a counter-clockwise spiral, starting in the top right-hand corner:

DVNV VIII IIEC

In many ciphers much additional security is gained by a second transposition, but the margin of error is also considerably increased; and of course the number of times one may repeat the transposition process is limited by one's intellectual capacity.

This summary of variations has not been given with the object of pointing the way to complexity; *security* should be the sole aim of cryptography, and piling complication upon complication does not necessarily lead to that end. Indeed, complications more often defeat the purposes of the correspondents than those of the enemy.

In general, the simplest cipher that offers sufficient security to serve one's ends is the best, and in choosing a cipher one should be guided by the attendant circumstances. If a single message of a few words is to be sent and secrecy is required for but a few hours, a simple device will serve. If many messages are to be sent and may be intercepted, the cipher can much more easily be broken, and greater ingenuity must be exercised by the correspondents. As a matter of fact, if an expert analyst comes into possession of two messages of exactly the same length, no matter how complicated the method used, the cryptograms can be solved with comparative ease.

Although this is the case, transposition cipher systems are common in military usage because they have the great advantage of simplicity and speed, both in transmission and deciphering — matters of paramount importance where hundreds of messages daily are transmitted. Besides, when devised by professional cryptographers, transposition ciphers afford a high degree of security, and it is possible to substitute new keys and variations at intervals, all of which may be memorized, and not reduced to writing.

# IV

## *Substitution Ciphers*

We have now reached the second of the two principles underlying all types of cryptography. The ciphers of this class differ from those we have just examined in that the units composing the plain text retain their relative positions, but do not retain their identities. They are, in other words, based on the principle of substitution and not on transposition.

Substitution is the principle underlying many of the conveniences of present-day life. Although they are superficially baffling to the uninitiated, they are no more cryptic than is the Chinese language, which offers scarcely any mysteries at all to a native of Hong Kong.

For example, the words written below are utterly meaningless to some, while others read them at a glance:

..-.  ..  .-.  .  ..  -.  ....  ---  .-..  -..  .--.  .-..  .
.-  ...  .  ...  -  .-  -.  -..  -...  -.--

If we had devised this cipher ourselves and given its key to only a few friends, then we should indeed have a cryptogram. But since it was devised by Morse and adopted by the world at large as the Continental code, we have only an excellent example of the substitution method. Anything but secrecy is the aim of this message: "Fire in hold. Please stand by."

Another substitution system universally employed in commerce is used by hundreds of office workers with remarkable facility. To the average executive, with his highly intellectual ignorance, it is baffling. If he pulled from the basket a crumpled piece of paper tossed wistfully into it by his weary stenographer, and found written on it these grotesque symbols, the poetic sadness of her message would be lost to him:

Transcribed it reads, "All for a handful of silver, all for a ribbon to pin on my coat . . ."

However, our purpose is not to discuss established systems of substitution, but to analyze methods for devising systems whose object is secret communication.

What is substituted for the letters of the alphabet, provided the same substitute is always used in a single message, is, in theory, quite immaterial. One may use playing cards; pictures; dots and dashes; arms, flags, or lanterns, as in semaphoring; or any variety of symbols or hieroglyphs. But in practice there are serious limitations. For instance, in devising the example of symbol substitution given below, we are placed under compulsion, by the facilities of our printer, to use only symbols that appear in his type book. Thus with the printer's convenience in mind we can prepare alphabetical equivalents:

| | | | | | |
|---|---|---|---|---|---|
| A | “ | J | ∧ | S | % |
| B | ( | K | ↓ | T | ¢ |
| C | ; | L | ♡ | U | & |
| D | + | M | ? | V | ♧ |
| E | ! | N | $ | W | ρ |
| F | / | O | : | X | ʃ |
| G | # | P | ' | Y | .. |
| H | @ | Q | ◇ | Z | ‿ |
| I | ) | R | • | | |

Using this key we can translate what looks like a printer's holiday greeting:

' " * % ) ? : $ ) : & %
P A R S I M O N I O U S

' * ) $ ¢ ! *
P R I N T E R

Although such a cipher text has a very cryptic appearance, it has limitations. We cannot transmit it by either wireless or telegraph, and, what is equally serious, we ourselves would find it very difficult to memorize the twenty-six equivalents. These same limitations, in fact, are universally applicable to symbol-substitution ciphers. However, other substitution methods provide equal security, and can be easily remembered and transmitted.

It becomes immediately apparent, when one realizes that substitution ciphers are broken only by the application of letter-frequency tests, that a symbol such as ! substituted for E offers no more security than is given by substituting another letter — W, for example. If the sign ! occurs with high frequency in a message, it is as easily recognized as E or W would be if it occurred with equal frequency, because E is the letter of highest frequency in the English language. Thus, by substituting different letters instead of symbols we have equal security and also obtain a cipher text that can be transmitted in any manner. We can arbitrarily use T for A, R for B, X for C, and so on, or we can write the letters of the alphabet on twenty-six bits of paper, jumble them in a hat, and declare that the first withdrawn will equal A, the second, B, and so forth, somewhat in the manner of the draft selection. In this way we would obtain some such alphabet as that shown below:

Plain: *A B C D E F G H I J K L M N O P Q R S T U V W X Y Z*

Cipher: B Z H K A X L Q J C G M U Y W I V D F R T S O E P N

This high-hat method would serve as well as any — and, as a matter of fact, it affords the maximum amount of security attainable by simple alphabetical substitution — but it is somewhat difficult to memorize the resulting cipher alphabet. In other words, it has the same limitation as the symbol substitution. Naturally, to decipher a message, a deciphering alphabet must be prepared. This is done by putting the cipher alphabet in actual alphabetical order with the normal equivalent beneath it; just the reverse of what is done above. Since many cipher users (espionage agents, for example) must not retain their keys in writing, we must consider the various memory aids that can be used, just as we did in discussing transposition encipherment.

Broadly speaking, there are three methods of substitution encipherment that enable one to produce a cipher alphabet mechanically. The first is single alphabet substitution, which includes the examples so far given: each plain-text letter is replaced by *only one* and *always the same* cipher equivalent.

The simplest method for making such a cipher alphabet is to represent the letter of the normal alphabet by the letter immediately following. A cipher of this type was used by Julius Caesar, who chose the third letter following as his substitute. Thus his alphabet was:

Plain: *A B C D E F G H I K L M N O P Q R S T V X Y Z*

Cipher: D E F G H I K L M N O P Q R S T V X Y Z A B C

(In Latin the letters J, U, and W were not used.) Had Caesar written his *Commentaries* in cipher, the opening sentence would read

KDOOMD HXY RPQMX GMZMXD MQ SDVYHX YVHX

instead of

*GALLIA EST OMNIS DIVISA IN PARTES TRES*

This method of encipherment offers, of course, practically

no security, and reveals a surprising naïveté in the author of the *Commentaries.*

It should be noticed that the great weakness of this method is that the cipher alphabet is in normal sequence. The shifting of the coincidence of the alphabets, either to left or right, does not change the order of the letters, and furthermore the

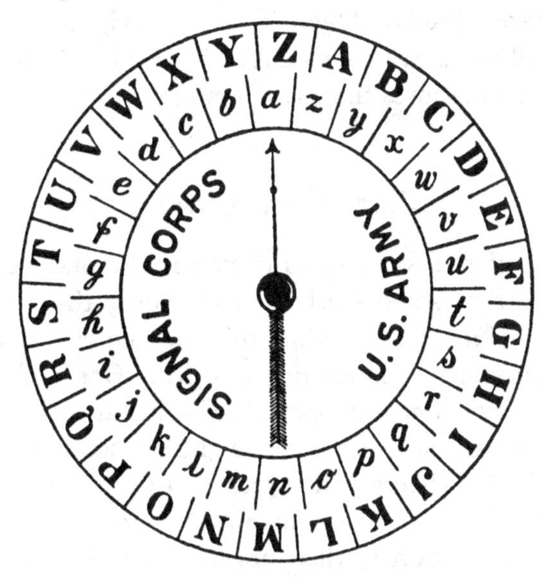


CIPHER WHEEL

equivalence in every case is reciprocal; that is, if A in the normal alphabet equals D in the cipher, then D in the cipher equals A in the normal alphabet. Although twenty-five different cipher alphabets may be formed by this method, these defects preclude its use for serious purposes. The twenty-five different ciphers are made conveniently available by a cipher wheel, two alphabet disks held by a center pivot. The upper and smaller disk can be turned to twenty-six points of coincidence. One of them, however, coincides with the normal alphabet.

A cipher that is a little less obvious can be made by reversing the alphabet in one of the disks, as illustrated above. At one of the twenty-six possible positions, the disks show this cipher:

Plain: *A B C D E F G H I J K L M N O P Q R S T U V W X Y Z*

Cipher: Z Y X W V U T S R Q P O N M L K J I H G F E D C B A

In this way twenty-six alphabets can be formed, but they all have the same disadvantage. They are reciprocal. If A equals Z, Z will still equal A, reciprocally. Moreover, the identification of two letters discloses the entire system.

## Mixed Cipher Systems

In view of the weaknesses of unmixed cipher sequences, it is apparent that some method of changing the sequence mechanically — but still according to a method that may be committed to memory — is highly desirable. One such method is to employ a key word or phrase. For instance, in attempting to attain greater SECURITY, we might choose that comforting word itself. Its letters will represent the first eight letters of our cipher alphabet. The remaining letters of the alphabet we shall then write down in their normal order, *omitting those that have already been used in the word* SECURITY.

Plain: *A B C D E F G H I J K L M N O P Q R S T U V W X Y Z*

Cipher: S E C U R I T Y A B D F G H J K L M N O P Q V W X Z

By this expedient we have produced a systematically mixed alphabet that does in fact present moderate — but only *very* moderate — security. Those who have the patience to experiment in amateur cryptography will with like patience be able, even without knowledge of the key word, to decipher any cryptogram employing a similarly mixed alphabet. The weakness is twofold. First, the key word itself will gradually become apparent, as the cryptanalyst works on the message. The reason for this will be evident after the section on analysis of substitution ciphers has been read (pages 98–113). Secondly, although none of the letters in the derived alphabet except Z remains in its original position, the sequence starting at A, B, is close to normal, being interrupted but eight times. Even should we reverse the sequence of the normal alphabet after the key word, so that it would read:

S E C U R I T Y Z X W V Q
P O N M L K J H G F D B A

the increase in security would be negligible, if it existed at all. Nor is anything really gained if we change the coincidence by shifting the key word to a position within the alphabet:

G F D B A S E C U R I T Y
Z X W V Q P O N M L K J H

We must look, therefore, for means of destroying the identity of the key word and the near-normal sequence of the letters following it.

## Transposition Mixed Cipher Sequence

To the rescue comes the familiar principle of transposition, but with a new purpose. It is to jumble for us not the letters of the message, but those of the key word and the remaining letters of the alphabet. Any of the transposition schemes we have discussed may be used; however, columnar transposition does the job thoroughly and simply.

Again using the word SECURITY as the key, the remaining letters of the alphabet are written in the manner shown below:

S E C U R I T Y
A B D F G H J K
L M N O P Q V W
X Z

Now we may transcribe vertically, deriving the cipher alphabet:

Plain: *A B C D E F G H I J K L M N O P Q R S T U V W X Y Z*

Cipher: S A L X E B M Z C D N U F O R G P I H Q T J V Y K W

Or again, if we wish to consider SECURITY as a numerical key as well as a key word, we should proceed by transcribing each column in its numerical order as it occurs in the word: C, the lowest in the alphabet, being 1; E, the next lowest, 2, and so forth.

| 5 | 2 | 1 | 7 | 4 | 3 | 6 | 8 |
|---|---|---|---|---|---|---|---|
| S | E | C | U | R | I | T | Y |
| A | B | D | F | G | H | J | K |
| L | M | N | O | P | Q | V | W |
| X | Z | | | | | | |

Plain: *A B C D E F G H I J K L M N O P Q R S T U V W X Y Z*

Cipher: C D N E B M Z I H Q R G P S A L X T J V U F O Y K W

This disarrangement of the alphabetical sequence is now as complete as could be desired. Although it has been done systematically, so that an enciphering and deciphering alphabet can easily be prepared without recourse to written memoranda, as great a disorder has resulted as if we had used the random-selection method of taking letters out of a hat. There are numerous highly complicated systems of mixing alphabets, but fundamentally they provide no greater security than the method shown above, and they do greatly increase the margin of error.

Unfortunately, the security we have now attained is still relatively low. We have not yet reached the degree of obscurity that cannot be penetrated even by the amateur cryptographer.

## Single-alphabet Substitution with Variants

To express it bluntly, all the substitution ciphers so far discussed can easily be broken by letter frequency, if the message is reasonably long. Since the average frequency of every letter in the alphabet has long been established (see page 153), our object must be to conceal the true occurrence of the letters, either by varying the substitute or by using more than one cipher alphabet in a single text.

By using a variation of the substitution device described on page 17 we can derive a single-cipher alphabet (I = J) with no variants:

| | 2 | 3 | 5 | 4 | 1 |
|---|---|---|---|---|---|
| 1 | A | B | C | D | E |
| 2 | F | G | H | I | K |
| 3 | L | M | N | O | P |
| 4 | Q | R | S | T | U |
| 5 | V | W | X | Y | Z |

By blocking the alphabet and numbering the rows and columns, we can indicate the desired letter by a number composed of the column and row number where they cross; L = 23, O = 43, U = 14; or the number sequence 22, 23, 11, 11 would very definitely read FLEE. However, with a rectangle numbered with three figures in the horizontal rows, as in the following:

| | 1 | 2 | 3 | 4 | 5 | 6 | 7 | 8 | 9 |
|---|---|---|---|---|---|---|---|---|---|
| 9, 6, 3 | A | B | C | D | E | F | G | H | I |
| 8, 5, 2 | J | K | L | M | N | O | P | Q | R |
| 7, 4, 1 | S | T | U | V | W | X | Y | Z | |

we have three variants for each letter. A may be 19, 16, or 13; K = 28, 25, or 22; and even the word AUK, that favorite esoteric bird of the crossword puzzle fans, can be indicated 27 different ways:

| | | |
|---|---|---|
| 13–31–22 | 13–34–22 | 13–37–22 |
| 16–34–25 | 16–31–22 | 16–34–28 |
| 19–37–28 | 19–37–22 | 19–37–25 |
| 13–31–25 | 13–34–25 | 13–37–25 |
| 16–34–22 | 16–37–22 | 16–31–25 |
| 19–31–22 | 19–31–25 | 19–31–28 |
| 13–31–28 | 13–34–28 | 13–37–28 |
| 16–31–28 | 16–37–25 | 16–37–28 |
| 19–31–28 | 19–34–22 | 19–34–28 |

Though it may seem that such a choice offers quite enough variation, even in enciphering of a three-letter word, it should be noted that the empty cell — 91, 94, or 97 — offers three additional meaningless opportunities to bedevil the enemy.

Authorities agree that the letters of highest frequency in our language are E–T–O–A–N–I–R–S–H. It is therefore wise to disguise their comparative frequency in a message and at the same time apparently increase the comparative frequency of less common letters. This can be done by assigning more numbers to the row containing the high-frequency letters. Using the same system of substitution as above, six variants for these common letters can be charted as follows:

| | 1 | 2 | 3 | 4 | 5 | 6 | 7 | 8 | 9 |
|---|---|---|---|---|---|---|---|---|---|
| 4, 5, 6, 7, 8, 9 | E | T | O | A | N | I | R | S | H |
| 2, 3 | B | C | D | F | G | J | K | L | M |
| 1 | P | Q | U | V | W | X | Y | Z | |

Another device that offers four variants for each letter is worthy of attention. It employs pairs of figures from 00 to 99. As these pairs are to be written in four rows, a key word must be chosen to govern the abnormality of their sequence. OUCH (which the *Oxford English Dictionary* defines as [archaic] "a clasp or buckle, often jewelled") will serve the purpose. To use this plan the cryptographer writes OUCH vertically and writes the normal alphabet (with I equalling both I and J) horizontally above it, beginning one column to the right:

| | *A* | *B* | *C* | *D* | *E* | *F* | *G* | *H* | *I* | *K* | *L* | *M* | *N* | *O* | *P* | *Q* | *R* | *S* | *T* | *U* | *V* | *W* | *X* | *Y* | *Z* |
|---|---|---|---|---|---|---|---|---|---|---|---|---|---|---|---|---|---|---|---|---|---|---|---|---|---|
| O | | | | | | | | | | | | | | | | | | | | | | | | | |
| U | | | | | | | | | | | | | | | | | | | | | | | | | |
| C | | | | | | | | | | | | | | | | | | | | | | | | | |
| H | | | | | | | | | | | | | | | | | | | | | | | | | |

The number of pairs from 00 to 99 is 100. We divide these into four groups, 00–24, 25–49, 50–74, 75–99. Each group is to be inscribed on a row from left to right. In the first row the letter O of our key word tells us the starting point. The second group begins under U, and so on. Thus:

| | A | B | C | D | E | F | G | H | I | K | L | M | N | O | P | Q | R | S | T | U | V | W | X | Y | Z |
|---|---|---|---|---|---|---|---|---|---|---|---|---|---|---|---|---|---|---|---|---|---|---|---|---|---|
| O | 12 | 13 | 14 | 15 | 16 | 17 | 18 | 19 | 20 | 21 | 22 | 23 | 24 | *00* | 01 | 02 | 03 | 04 | 05 | 06 | 07 | 08 | 09 | 10 | 11 |
| U | 31 | 32 | 33 | 34 | 35 | 36 | 37 | 38 | 39 | 40 | 41 | 42 | 43 | 44 | 45 | 46 | 47 | 48 | 49 | *25* | 26 | 27 | 28 | 29 | 30 |
| C | 73 | 74 | *50* | 51 | 52 | 53 | 54 | 55 | 56 | 57 | 58 | 59 | 60 | 61 | 62 | 63 | 64 | 65 | 66 | 67 | 68 | 69 | 70 | 71 | 72 |
| H | 93 | 94 | 95 | 96 | 97 | 98 | 99 | *75* | 76 | 77 | 78 | 79 | 80 | 81 | 82 | 83 | 84 | 85 | 86 | 87 | 88 | 89 | 90 | 91 | 92 |

We then have sixty-four ways of writing THE, the commonest word in the English language, beginning with 05–19–16. We shall allow the reader to work out the remaining sixty-three ways to his own satisfaction.

In the final cipher text made by this system, as is the case in any system, security is increased by regrouping into units of five. If we encipher such an indisputable but seldom stated fact as

A L L M E N A R E M O R T A L
12–22–41 23–16–80 93–64–35 42–61–03–66–73–58

the final cryptogram would be

12224 12316 80936 43542 61036 67358

As has been previously stated, there are a great many variations of single-alphabet substitution, some of them enormously complicated. For instance, one may substitute a number of three or four digits instead of two for a single letter, and again one can assign letter equivalents for the cipher digits and, by changing the numerical text back into an alphabetical text, add an encipherment step to the system. But since we have described the basic methods, little will be accomplished by multiplying examples, and further ramifications can safely be left to the reader's imagination.

We have now reached a point where our enciphering systems have become fairly complicated. The complications, of course, in turn make the methods used to break the ciphers more complex. Since we are going to demonstrate very shortly (see Polyalphabetic Ciphers, page 73) how such systems are broken, we shall at this time only hint how they are exposed, our purpose at present being to point out their inherent weakness and to devise a way to eliminate it.

If a sufficient number of cipher messages are intercepted and are subjected to a thorough analysis, certain repetitions will ultimately be discovered. Single digits or letters, or groups of them, will appear at intervals and in juxtapositions that will betray the system. This weakness is innate in the system itself. It is accentuated, moreover, by the very nature of man. Just as we unconsciously form preferences for certain words and, without being aware of it, fall into the habit of using set phrases, so the hurried cryptographic clerk may, either through negligence or haste, repeat the same variant or subconsciously follow the same method of selection so that his manner of variation is revealed by its constancy. The cadence is detected; the cipher broken.

Perhaps this human tendency to the habitual will help us to discern the difference between polyalphabetic substitution and single-alphabet substitution with variants, since it is that tendency or weakness of habit that the polyalphabetic method aims to correct.

At first sight we should suppose that the table on page 67 represents a poly- or multiple-alphabetic system of substitution. It is undeniable that it contains four different cipher alphabets. But the choice of cipher character to be used is left entirely to the discretion of the person who does the enciphering. It is therefore chosen at random. In a true polyalphabetic enciphering system, one is under compulsion by the nature of the method to use a definite character. Whether or not this attains the end it is designed to meet — namely, that of correcting the all too human weakness of the cipher clerk — depends to a large extent upon the skill of the man who fashions the system. If it seems paradoxical that the weakness of repetition can be alleviated by repetition — and we admit it to be so — we can only suggest that some systems are better than others, and that it is sometimes preferable to leap from the frying pan into the fire. So we shall proceed to explore the land of true polyalphabetic substitution to see if we can find a systematic method that makes it more difficult to discover the recurrence of an offending variant.

## Polyalphabetic Substitution

One of the commonest systems of substitution encipherment with several alphabets can be demonstrated by the following example.

We use SHIPWRECK as the key word. It gives the key number:

```
S H I P W R E C K
8 3 4 6 9 7 2 1 5
```

The message is in the form of a query:

*IS THERE SAFETY IN NUMBERS*

The first step is to write the message underneath the key:

```
8 3 4 6 9 7 2 1 5
I S T H E R E S A
F E T Y I N N U M
B E R S
```

The number at the top of each column determines the selection of the letter to be substituted for the letters in that column.

For the first column, the eighth letter following I, F, and B respectively, is to be used — that is, Q (the eighth letter after I), N (the eighth after F), and J (the eighth letter after B). For the second column, the third letters succeeding the letters in the column are substituted — V, H, and H. It is well to keep the normal alphabet displayed for convenience while enciphering.

A B C D E F G H I J K L M N O P Q R S T U V W X Y Z

When the entire message has been enciphered with the proper substitutes we have:

| 8 | 3 | 4 | 6 | 9 | 7 | 2 | 1 | 5 |
|---|---|---|---|---|---|---|---|---|
| Q | V | X | N | N | Y | G | T | F |
| N | H | X | E | R | U | P | V | R |
| J | H | V | Y | | | | | |

If now we write the cipher text in eleven two-letter groups we have:

QV XN NY GT FN HX ER UP VR JH VY

In the process of writing this cryptogram we have used nine different cipher alphabets. This fact will be immediately apparent when we study the Vigenère table given on page 71.

In this table twenty-five substitution alphabets for the normal alphabet on the top line have been formed. Our key number 834697215 (or word) SHIPWRECK, told us to use the first nine and the exact order in which to use them. In row 8, Q is indicated as the substitute for I; in row 3, V is found under S; and so on. It will be noticed that the alphabets in the Vigenère table have been slid successively one letter to the left. In other words, they begin successively one letter, two letters, three letters after A. In our message IS THERE SAFETY IN NUMBERS, we obtain exactly the same result by substituting the letter found at the intersections of the columns headed by our plain text letters IS THERE, and so on, with the rows designated by the digits of our key number 834697215. The two procedures are equivalent. If we look down column I we shall find, where it crosses row 8, the letter Q; at the intersection of column S with row 3 is the letter V, and so forth, these being the eighth and third letters respectively after I and S in the normal alphabet.

It will be recalled that such alphabets as those in the Vige-

VIGENÈRE TABLE

| | | | | | | | | | | | | | | | | | | | | | | | | | | |
|---|---|---|---|---|---|---|---|---|---|---|---|---|---|---|---|---|---|---|---|---|---|---|---|---|---|---|
| 0 | A | B | C | D | E | F | G | H | I | J | K | L | M | N | O | P | Q | R | S | T | U | V | W | X | Y | Z |
| 1 | B | C | D | E | F | G | H | I | J | K | L | M | N | O | P | Q | R | S | T | U | V | W | X | Y | Z | A |
| 2 | C | D | E | F | G | H | I | J | K | L | M | N | O | P | Q | R | S | T | U | V | W | X | Y | Z | A | B |
| 3 | D | E | F | G | H | I | J | K | L | M | N | O | P | Q | R | S | T | U | V | W | X | Y | Z | A | B | C |
| 4 | E | F | G | H | I | J | K | L | M | N | O | P | Q | R | S | T | U | V | W | X | Y | Z | A | B | C | D |
| 5 | F | G | H | I | J | K | L | M | N | O | P | Q | R | S | T | U | V | W | X | Y | Z | A | B | C | D | E |
| 6 | G | H | I | J | K | L | M | N | O | P | Q | R | S | T | U | V | W | X | Y | Z | A | B | C | D | E | F |
| 7 | H | I | J | K | L | M | N | O | P | Q | R | S | T | U | V | W | X | Y | Z | A | B | C | D | E | F | G |
| 8 | I | J | K | L | M | N | O | P | Q | R | S | T | U | V | W | X | Y | Z | A | B | C | D | E | F | G | H |
| 9 | J | K | L | M | N | O | P | Q | R | S | T | U | V | W | X | Y | Z | A | B | C | D | E | F | G | H | I |
| 10 | K | L | M | N | O | P | Q | R | S | T | U | V | W | X | Y | Z | A | B | C | D | E | F | G | H | I | J |
| 11 | L | M | N | O | P | Q | R | S | T | U | V | W | X | Y | Z | A | B | C | D | E | F | G | H | I | J | K |
| 12 | M | N | O | P | Q | R | S | T | U | V | W | X | Y | Z | A | B | C | D | E | F | G | H | I | J | K | L |
| 13 | N | O | P | Q | R | S | T | U | V | W | X | Y | Z | A | B | C | D | E | F | G | H | I | J | K | L | M |
| 14 | O | P | Q | R | S | T | U | V | W | X | Y | Z | A | B | C | D | E | F | G | H | I | J | K | L | M | N |
| 15 | P | Q | R | S | T | U | V | W | X | Y | Z | A | B | C | D | E | F | G | H | I | J | K | L | M | N | O |
| 16 | Q | R | S | T | U | V | W | X | Y | Z | A | B | C | D | E | F | G | H | I | J | K | L | M | N | O | P |
| 17 | R | S | T | U | V | W | X | Y | Z | A | B | C | D | E | F | G | H | I | J | K | L | M | N | O | P | Q |
| 18 | S | T | U | V | W | X | Y | Z | A | B | C | D | E | F | G | H | I | J | K | L | M | N | O | P | Q | R |
| 19 | T | U | V | W | X | Y | Z | A | B | C | D | E | F | G | H | I | J | K | L | M | N | O | P | Q | R | S |
| 20 | U | V | W | X | Y | Z | A | B | C | D | E | F | G | H | I | J | K | L | M | N | O | P | Q | R | S | T |
| 21 | V | W | X | Y | Z | A | B | C | D | E | F | G | H | I | J | K | L | M | N | O | P | Q | R | S | T | U |
| 22 | W | X | Y | Z | A | B | C | D | E | F | G | H | I | J | K | L | M | N | O | P | Q | R | S | T | U | V |
| 23 | X | Y | Z | A | B | C | D | E | F | G | H | I | J | K | L | M | N | O | P | Q | R | S | T | U | V | W |
| 24 | Y | Z | A | B | C | D | E | F | G | H | I | J | K | L | M | N | O | P | Q | R | S | T | U | V | W | X |
| 25 | Z | A | B | C | D | E | F | G | H | I | J | K | L | M | N | O | P | Q | R | S | T | U | V | W | X | Y |

nère table (if there is no change in the normal sequence of the letters) are reciprocal, and that even though we reverse the order of the letters the alphabets will still remain reciprocal. The poor security afforded by reciprocal alphabets has already been mentioned. The greater security of a disarranged sequence has been emphasized. If the polyalphabetic substitution system just described appears to have some security (in fact, it has very little) then logical reasoning suggests that a table of twenty-six alphabets each systematically disarranged will have greater security.

Below we have constructed such a table, and enciphered a message using more than one of its alphabets.

We have chosen the word ENIGMAS as our key word for the disarrangement, and GAS for the key to the alphabets used. We shall form twenty-six alphabets by sliding each one consecutively one space to the right. Our message, THIS IS THOROUGHLY INSIDIOUS, is written in five letter groups:

THISI STHOR OUGHL YINSI DIOUS

and we make an alphabetic table using our key word ENIGMAS as a starting point, and marking the alphabets or rows to be used as designated by our key word GAS.

| | E | N | I | G | M | A | S | B | C | D | F | H | J | K | L | O | P | Q | R | T | U | V | W | X | Y | Z |
|---|---|---|---|---|---|---|---|---|---|---|---|---|---|---|---|---|---|---|---|---|---|---|---|---|---|---|
| | N | I | G | M | A | S | B | C | D | F | H | J | K | L | O | P | Q | R | T | U | V | W | X | Y | Z | E |
| | I | G | M | A | S | B | C | D | F | H | J | K | L | O | P | Q | R | T | U | V | W | X | Y | Z | E | N |
| G | G | M | A | S | B | C | D | F | H | J | K | L | O | P | Q | R | T | U | V | W | X | Y | Z | E | N | I |
| | M | A | S | B | C | D | F | H | J | K | L | O | P | Q | R | T | U | V | W | X | Y | Z | E | N | I | G |
| A | A | S | B | C | D | F | H | J | K | L | O | P | Q | R | T | U | V | W | X | Y | Z | E | N | I | G | M |
| S | S | B | C | D | F | H | J | K | L | O | P | Q | R | T | U | V | W | X | Y | Z | E | N | I | G | M | A |

We then write the word GAS repeatedly beneath our plain text, and beneath these repetitions the letters of our cipher text.

THISI STHOR OUGHL YINSI DIOUS
*GASGA SGASG ASGAS GASGA SGASG*

Thus at the intersection of column T and row G we find cipher letter W; column H, row A, gives P; column I, row S, gives C; column S, row G, gives D; and so on.

| | |
|---|---|
| Plain: | THISI STHOR OUGHL YINSI DIOUS |
| | *GASGA SGASG ASGAS GASGA SGASG* |
| Cipher: | WPCDB JWPVV UESPU NBBDB OAUED |

We must admit that unless we had chosen our message and key very carefully, with malice aforethought, the decipherment would be virtually impossible unless one of the key words were known. However, we did choose it purposely to demonstrate the principles upon which such a cipher system could infallibly be broken if the text were long enough, or if there were more messages to provide an extensive table of frequencies. The logic of this will be revealed after the outline — for it can be no more — of the cryptanalytic process. This outline will show the basic method of approach to all such cryptographic problems, and will save the reader the reading of many pages of dry schedules.

WPCDB JWPVV UESPU NBBDB OAUED

It will be noticed that three different pairs of letters occur twice in the cipher text. The interval between the first and second occurrence of WP is six letters; between the two occurrences of DB, fifteen letters; between those of UE, twelve letters. Thus we have repetitions after intervals of 6, 15, and 12. This set of intervals may be due to mere coincidence or it may be due to the nature of the system employed. We shall assume that the latter is the case here — which, of course, it is.

The factors of 6 are 2 and 3; of 15, 3 and 5; of 12, 3 and 4.

From the fact that the common factor is 3 we assume that three alphabets have been used in the encipherment. The reason for this assumption will become clearer if we arrange our two texts as follows:

| Cipher text | | | Plain text | | |
|---|---|---|---|---|---|
| G | A | S | G | A | S |
| **W** | **P** | C | **T** | **H** | I |
| **D** | **B** | J | **S** | **I** | S |
| **W** | **P** | V | **T** | **H** | O |
| V | **U** | **E** | R | **O** | **U** |
| S | P | U | G | H | L |
| N | B | B | Y | I | N |
| **D** | **B** | O | **S** | **I** | D |
| A | **U** | **E** | I | **O** | **U** |
| D | | | S | | |

Notice that the positions of the repetitions of TH, SI, and OU in the plain text correspond exactly with those of WP, DB, and UE in the cipher text. They are respectively separated by an interval of 3, or some multiple of 3. If we employ seven different alphabets to encipher a message which contains repeated combinations of letters or words separated by an interval of 7 or a multiple of 7, then obviously the repetition will occur correspondingly in the cipher text. The more alphabets we use the greater are the chances against such repetitions, but even though twenty-six alphabets are used, repetitions are bound to occur in voluminous correspondence, and it is by the method described above that such systems may be broken.

Having established the number of alphabets used in the cipher correspondence, the analyst writes the text in columns as above, the number of columns being the same as the number of alphabets employed. Having in this way classified each cipher character according to its alphabet, he sets about to determine its plain-text equivalent. If the cipher text is sufficiently long the correct equivalent will be found by using tables of letter frequency. As this analytical method is discussed in some detail in the chapter on cryptanalysis of substitution ciphers, we shall omit it here, and assume the analyst has correctly determined the equivalents, so they may be written in their proper sequence in the various cipher alphabets.

1. G M A S B C D F H J K L O P Q R T U V W X Y Z E N I

2. A S B C D F H J K L O P Q R T U V W X Y Z E N I G M

3. S B C D F H J K L O P Q R T U V W X Y Z E N I G M A

Even a casual examination discloses the key words GAS and ENIGMAS. The table from which we did our enciphering can now be constructed. And should the analyst be required to decipher any further texts based on this system, he would need only to discover the key word designating the alphabets to be used.

The ease with which the key words GAS and ENIGMAS can be identified is a disadvantage that should and can easily be corrected by using a systematically but thoroughly mixed alphabet such as was described on pages 63–4. To an expert cryptanalyst, however, the security attained even in this system is negligible. Its weakness lies basically in the phenomena of a cyclic or periodic nature which manifest themselves externally in the cipher text. These phenomena are due to the repeated key word or words. Their manifestations can be disguised or modified in various ways, some of which expressed briefly are these: (1) an invariable key may be applied to letter groupings of variable length in the plain text; (2) a variable key may be applied to fixed groupings of letters; (3) variable keys may be applied to variable groupings; (4) successive letters after the initial letter of the cipher text or plain text may indicate the key letter to be used; (5) the entire cipher text resulting from a polyalphabetic substitution system using a variable key applied to variable plain-text groupings may be re-enciphered by transposition methods. Thus all the agonies of both systems are combined for the cryptanalyst.

## Mechanical Devices

Today the senders and receivers of cipher messages are to be found almost exclusively in the personnel of our armed forces. The military prerequisites for secret communication, according to our War Department, are: (1) simplicity, rapidity, practicability; (2) secrecy; (3) accuracy; (4) economy. In the combat zone, nerves are taut. Who at moments of great tension could cope with the complications mentioned above, either in enciphering or deciphering? Serious errors would be made even if the encipherer were not pressed for time and could work at leisure. In such circumstances secrecy would probably be so complete that neither friend nor foe would share the secret with the enciphering clerk.

In the combat zone, obviously, a degree of security must

be sacrificed for accuracy and rapidity of transmission. In this spot the armchair cryptographer is no more helpful than the armchair strategist: for, after all, in the zone of combat, time is of the essence of the undertaking. Too little knowledge or knowledge too late is worthless. For these reasons a mechanical cipher device was of practical value in the Second World War. This device is virtually the same as that invented in 1891 by Bazeries, who in turn took the idea in whole cloth from Thomas Jefferson.

The enciphering mechanism is little more than a convenient device for using a mixed-alphabet Vigenère table. There are twenty-five disks in the modern Army cryptograph (twenty in the original Bazeries machine) that fit snugly around a cylindrical shaft. On the rim of each disk, which is removable, is stamped a different disarranged alphabet of twenty-six letters. The disks are numbered on their sides (1–25) and lettered (B–Z) so that the order in which they are to be assembled on the shaft may be designated — either numerically or alphabetically — by a key word or its numerical equivalent (see page 49). To an additional blank disk is attached a guide rule, which may be revolved about the shaft and which serves the same purpose as a ruler when the latter is used with a multiple mixed alphabet table. (The Bazeries device did not have a guide rule.) Lugs and slots on the disks enable the operator to lock them on the cylinder in any relative position desired.

To encipher a message, the disks are arranged in the order predetermined by a key word or phrase. This can conveniently be done by using a graph paper having quarter-inch squares. On the top line the squares are numbered 1–25 from left to right. Then, beginning at the left, the key word or phrase is written repeatedly on the line below until all the squares in the lower line are filled. If the key phrase is STRIKE AT DAWN, the first two steps will give:

| 1 | 2 | 3 | 4 | 5 | 6 | 7 | 8 | 9 | 10 | 11 | 12 | 13 | 14 | 15 | 16 | 17 | 18 | 19 | 20 | 21 | 22 | 23 | 24 | 25 |
|---|---|---|---|---|---|---|---|---|---|---|---|---|---|---|---|---|---|---|---|---|---|---|---|---|
| S | T | R | I | K | E | A | T | D | A | W | N | S | T | R | I | K | E | A | T | D | A | W | N | S |

Next, directly below the letters of the key sequence, each letter is numbered according to its relative position in the normal alphabet, just as is done in columnar transposition (page 48). When the same letter occurs two or more times in the key sequence, the square under which it occurs the first time is numbered as indicated above; the square under that in which it appears the second time is given the next higher number, and so on. Thus we complete the third step as follows:

| 1 | 2 | 3 | 4 | 5 | 6 | 7 | 8 | 9 | 10 | 11 | 12 | 13 | 14 | 15 | 16 | 17 | 18 | 19 | 20 | 21 | 22 | 23 | 24 | 25 |
|---|---|---|---|---|---|---|---|---|---|---|---|---|---|---|---|---|---|---|---|---|---|---|---|---|
| S | T | R | I | K | E | A | T | D | A | W | N | S | T | R | I | K | E | A | T | D | A | W | N | S |
| 17 | 20 | 15 | 9 | 11 | 7 | 1 | 21 | 5 | 2 | 24 | 13 | 18 | 22 | 16 | 10 | 12 | 8 | 3 | 23 | 6 | 4 | 25 | 14 | 19 |

In this way the key phrase on the second line gives the numeral key on the third line and the disks are put on the cylinder in the order indicated by it. Disk 17 is put on first, 20 next, then 15, and so forth.

The disks, now on the cylinder, are revolved so that the first 25 letters of the plain-text message that is to be sent are spelled out from left to right along the guide rule. Then the disks are locked in that position on the cylinder. Across the disks we may read 26 rows of letters. We have used one for the plain-text message. Of the remaining 25, any one that is not concealed by the guide rule may be used for the cipher text of the first 25 etters of the message. After one of them has been selected the cipher letter sequence is written down, the cylinders are loosened so that they can be revolved, and the next and succeeding 25-letter groups of the message are enciphered in the same way, except that each time the operation is made a different cipher row is used.

In order to decipher the message, the receiver of it arranges the disks on his cylinder according to the key word, just as did the sender. He then writes down the cipher messages, 25 letters to the line, on cross-section paper and turns the disks so that the row above the guide rule repeats the ciphertext letters. Having locked the disks in position, he examines the other rows until he finds one that reads intelligibly; there will be only one such row. After writing the portion of the message deciphered beneath the first 25 letters of the cipher text on the cross-section paper, he continues with the rest.

It has been estimated that the security of messages enciphered by this method is from six hours to three days. In consequence, the key must be changed very frequently according to a plan previously agreed upon. Such a plan involves not only an ordered sequence of keys successively to be used, but the predetermination of the exact moment when a new key is to be substituted.

## Variations of Vigenère

In this discussion of substitution encipherment, we have pointed out the inherent weakness of the Vigenère system, devised in the sixteenth century, and traced the progressive elimination of its weaknesses and those inherent in the remedies, until we reached the point of maximum practical security. In doing so we have purposefully omitted mention of certain cryptographers who are discussed at length in works more concerned with the history and background of cryptography. Although significant in their own times, their work has for the most part been but modification of the Vigenère system, and has offered negligible if any security beyond that of Vigenère. For those interested, a few of the most famous of these systems are briefly discussed below.

More than a century before Vigenère, Giovanni Battista della Porta (*c.* 1538–1615) devised a cipher table of 12 alphabets (see p. 79). It is possible that this system was the inspiration of the Vigenère table. In it the letters of the second half of the alphabet are written in their proper order directly under the letters of the first half, to form the first cipher alphabet. Foreshadowing the Vigenère method, the succeeding alphabets

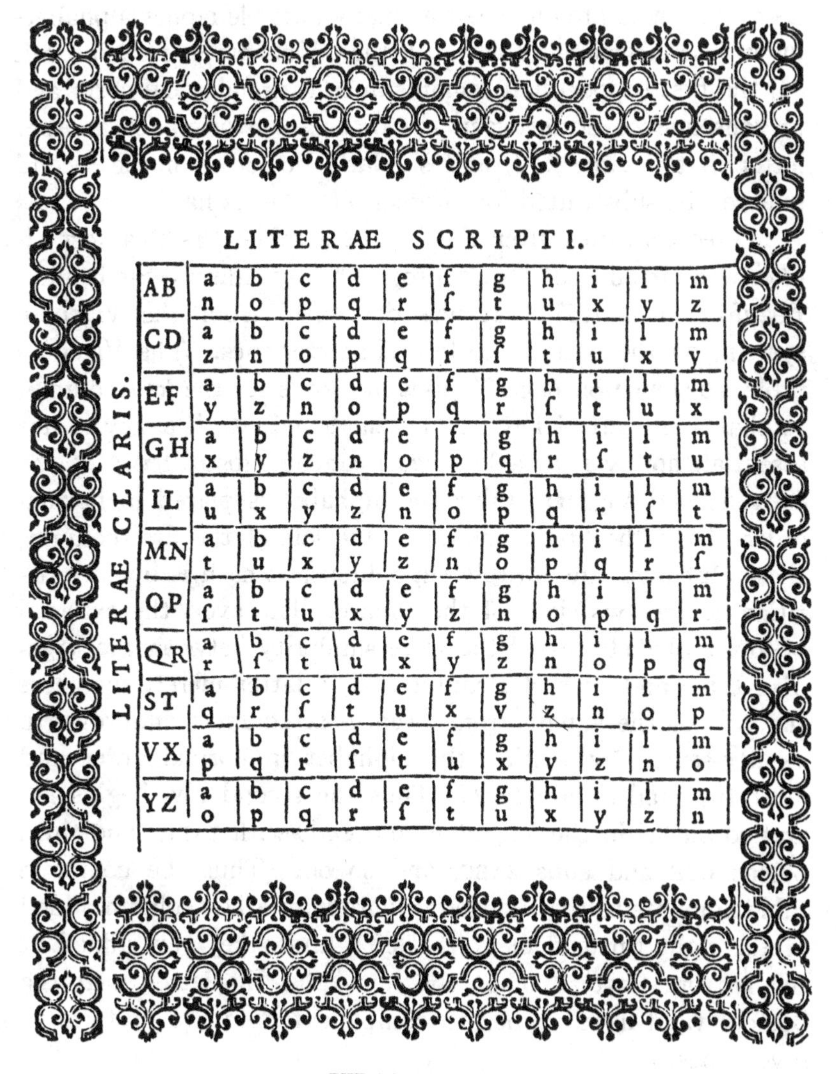

LITERAE SCRIPTI.

LITERAE CLARIS.

| | | | | | | | | | | | |
|---|---|---|---|---|---|---|---|---|---|---|---|
| AB | a | b | c | d | e | f | g | h | i | l | m |
| | n | o | p | q | r | ſ | t | u | x | y | z |
| CD | a | b | c | d | e | f | g | h | i | l | m |
| | z | n | o | p | q | r | ſ | t | u | x | y |
| EF | a | b | c | d | e | f | g | h | i | l | m |
| | y | z | n | o | p | q | r | ſ | t | u | x |
| GH | a | b | c | d | e | f | g | h | i | l | m |
| | x | y | z | n | o | p | q | r | ſ | t | u |
| IL | a | b | c | d | e | f | g | h | i | l | m |
| | u | x | y | z | n | o | p | q | r | ſ | t |
| MN | a | b | c | d | e | f | g | h | i | l | m |
| | t | u | x | y | z | n | o | p | q | r | ſ |
| OP | a | b | c | d | e | f | g | h | i | l | m |
| | ſ | t | u | x | y | z | n | o | p | q | r |
| QR | a | b | c | d | c | f | g | h | i | l | m |
| | r | ſ | t | u | x | y | z | n | o | p | q |
| ST | a | b | c | d | e | f | g | h | i | l | m |
| | q | r | ſ | t | u | x | v | z | n | o | p |
| VX | a | b | c | d | e | f | g | h | i | l | m |
| | p | q | r | ſ | t | u | x | y | z | n | o |
| YZ | a | b | c | d | e | f | g | h | i | l | m |
| | o | p | q | r | ſ | t | u | x | y | z | n |

THE PORTA TABLE

are formed by sliding the second half backwards under the first half, which remains constant. A key determines which cipher is to be used. The defects of this table will readily be seen: (1) there are only half as many possible cipher alphabets as in the Vigenère table; (2) the alphabets are reciprocal; (3) the first (upper) half remains in true alphabetical order and in consequence no letter in it can be substituted for another letter in the same half, and similarly no letter of the second half can be substituted for another letter in its half.

Three centuries after the Vigenère table, the Beaufort cipher was introduced into cryptography by Admiral Sir Francis Beaufort (1774–1857). It was developed from the Vigenère system, on the basis of certain characteristics. The Vigenère table, as shown on page 71, uses numerals for the key column, so that a numerical key can be employed; such a key is not essential, however, as a key word can be substituted. In the conventional Vigenère table the alphabet is placed in normal order above the first row and to the left of the first column; these alphabets are entirely superfluous, as each is but a repetition of the two sides of the square. However, the external or key alphabets reveal the close similarity between the Vigenère table and that of Beaufort. The latter merely increases the size of the square from twenty-six columns and rows to twenty-seven, by writing the alphabet in normal order and after the final Z, adding A. Thus the second row begins BC, and so on, as in the Vigenère, and ends with ZAB. The third begins CDE and ends ZABC, and so on. Thus the complete table amounts to the Vigenère square with a key column added at the right (instead of at the left), and a key row added at the bottom (instead of at the top), plus the letter A at the bottom right-hand corner to complete the square of twenty-seven lines.

Although Francis Beaufort did not really improve on the Vigenère table, he did devise a method of using it that eliminated one of its weaknesses — the reciprocal alphabets. When enciphering, instead of starting with the plain-text letter, Beaufort starts with the key letter, traces down the column from it until he comes to the plain-text letter, where he turns at right angles and follows along the row to the cipher letter at the end. (In the Beaufort table, the same letter occurs at both ends of each row and column.) In consequence he achieves nonreciprocal alphabets. This procedure can be demonstrated on the Vigenère table, page 71.[1]

RECIPROCAL METHOD

Plain-text M → Key *V* → Cipher J
Plain-text M ← Key *V* ← Cipher J

NONRECIPROCAL METHOD

Key *V* → Plain-text M → Cipher R
E (not M) ← Key *V* ← Cipher R

The absence of reciprocity does not, of course, prevent the cryptanalyst from breaking the cipher by letter frequency. The person primarily inconvenienced by the complication is the decipherer to whom the message is addressed.

Perhaps the fact that many systems of enciphering devised in modern times are but minor variations of the Vigenère table is best illustrated by reference to their equivalent slides. In its most elementary form, a slide is composed of two strips of paper placed one below the other. On the upper the letters of the alphabet are printed, spaced exactly the same distance apart. On the lower, two alphabets are printed, one following the other, and the letters are spaced at the same intervals apart as on the upper. The upper strip provides the plain-text letters and is theoretically stationary. The lower represents the cipher letters and slides in either direction.

Thus if the key is K, the lower strip is slid along until the K appears under A, and all the cipher equivalents to be used in enciphering will be found under the plain-text letter of the

[1] In substituting the Vigenère table for the Beaufort, it is necessary to turn left at the intersection of the columns and rows, since in it all four sides are not alike.

upper strip. In the famous Saint-Cyr slide (named for the French military academy) the alphabet on the upper strip is in normal order, as are the two alphabets on the lower strip. Thus by sliding the lower strip, twenty-six cipher alphabets can be formed. These alphabets are precisely the same as those formed in the Vigenère table. Slides similarly can be made for the Beaufort table, the Porta, and all other similar tables. They do not introduce any new elements that provide additional security, any more than does the revolving disk, shown on page 61. The disk has the advantage of making the repetition of the cipher alphabet unnecessary. Obviously

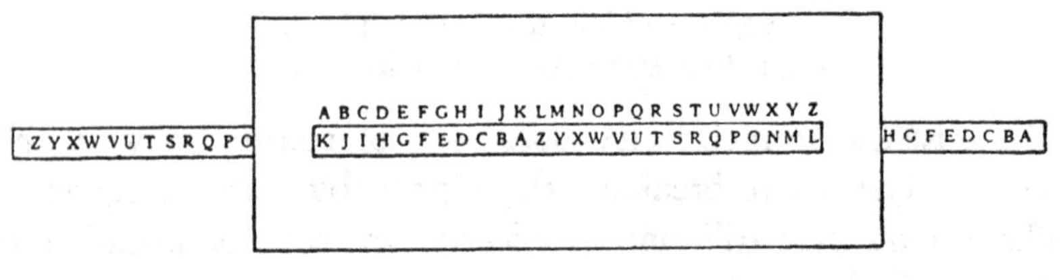


SLIDE

the cipher alphabets of the lower strip may be disarranged in accordance with any of the devices described above. Although slides present no new cryptographic problems, they are a great convenience both in enciphering and deciphering.

## Polygraph Substitution

A method that represents a distinct departure from Vigenère's, on the other hand, is found in polygraph substitution — that is, the substitution of cipher digraphs or trigraphs for the plain-text digraphs or trigraphs. There are a great many ways in which this substitution can be made but most of the devices necessitate the making of elaborate tables in which the 676 (26 × 26) two-letter combinations are placed, either alphabetically arranged or systematically disarranged. Then the plain-text alphabet is written above the top row of digraphs and again beside the first or last column. In doing this, the plain-text alphabets may once more be disarranged. To find the cipher digraph, one follows down the column above which the first letter of the plain-text digraph appears until one comes to the intersection with the row designated by the second letter of the digraph (or vice versa). The cipher digraph, of course, is the one found at the intersection. To decipher, the plain-text letters are found at the top of the column and at the end of the row.

Probably the most popular system of polygraph substitution currently is what is known as the Playfair cipher. It has the advantage over all other basically similar systems in not being in the least cumbersome; the key can easily be memorized and the processes of encipherment and decipherment are simple. Its principles are demonstrated in the following illustration:

As our key table we use a grille $5 \times 5$, and in it inscribe the alphabet in a spiral counterclockwise route, omitting Z (see H–4, page 43).

| | | | | |
|---|---|---|---|---|
| I | H | G | F | E |
| J | U | T | S | D |
| K | V | Y | R | C |
| L | W | X | Q | B |
| M | N | O | P | A |

Now, it is obvious that there are three and only three positions in which any two letters can be in respect to each other. They must be in the same row, in the same column, or at the diagonally opposite corners of a rectangle formed by the two rows and two columns in which the plain-text letters appear. IG are in the same row. FQ are in the same column. EK are at the diagonally opposite corners of the rectangle IECK.

With these three possibilities, the following rules for enciphering are arbitrarily established:

1. In enciphering digraphs in the same row, substitute the letter immediately to the right of each letter. For IG use HF.

2. For digraphs in the same column, use letters immediately beneath them. For FQ use SP.

3. For digraphs in a diagonally opposite relation, substitute the letters that appear at diagonally opposite corners of the rectangle beginning with the first plain-text letter and substituting the cipher letter found in the same row (not column). EK gives IC, not CI. For EY use GC, since we use the letter found in the same row, not column.

Obviously it is not always possible to follow these three rules. In attempting to apply rule 1 (plain-text letters in the same row), one of the letters may be found at the end of the row, so that no letter is to the right of it. In such a case we substitute the letter at the opposite end of the same row: for WB use XL; for MA use NM.

Similarly when enciphering two letters in the same column: for KM use LI; for HN use UH.

The application of rule 3 is always possible.

Inevitably there are weaknesses in this system.[1] Among the more apparent of them is the existence of one cipher digraph as a substitute for any given plain-text digraph. This weakness, when a table of digraph frequencies is used to break the cipher, is comparable to the weakness of a single-alphabet substitution encipherment, and the system offers considerably less security than was provided by the device by which we enciphered AUK on page 66. One way to obviate this weak-

[1] For a remarkably thorough discussion of the weaknesses of the Playfair cipher and of method for breaking it, see *Elementary Cryptanalysis*, by Helen Fouché Gaines.

ness would be to juxtapose four similar grilles and in each inscribe the alphabet by a different route. When enciphering, one could then use the four alphabets successively for each succeeding plain-text letter. However, the ultimate desideratum is security *without*, not *with*, too much complication.

A second defect of the Playfair system lies in the fact that when a plain-text digraph is reversed, the equivalent cipher digraph is reversed: if AM gives TS, then MA gives ST.

These two weaknesses in the system are fatal.

# V

## *Codes Compared with Ciphers*

We have taken advantage of the somewhat arbitrary distinction between codes and ciphers in the science of cryptography — for no true line of demarcation can be drawn between them — to exclude the former from our discussion. In this we are influenced not by any misconception in regard to the importance of codes, but by the fact that they have comparatively little interest for those who are engrossed in the mysteries of secret writing.

A code book is a dictionary — a bilingual dictionary. If we encounter a word *agua*, we can find that it means water. What is the substitute for "city"? *Ciudad.* Similarly, if we use a commercial or secret code book, we may learn that ZYNJE means water, and that we should encode EWLYP for city.

From this it is apparent that the distinction between codes and ciphers is arbitrary; for, after all, we are dealing with no more than a highly specialized form of substitution ciphering. The difference is technical. However, in the restricted meaning, ciphers employ disarranged letters or substitutions for letters, whereas codes employ substitutions (generally five-letter groups) for words, phrases, or sentences. Their use commercially is primarily for economy, since commercial code books are easily available. TSODS, meaning *Have considered the matter from all points of view*, or BOCKI, meaning *Do not arbitrate, if necessary submit to what is asked but endeavor to get some small advantage*, offers a considerable saving in expense.

Surprisingly enough, the normal alphabet with only six vowels can be permuted so that more than 100,000 five-letter groups can be formed into pronounceable "words," all differing from one another in at least two letters. In commercial telegraphy this difference is an important safeguard against error in transmission. The recent codes have further reduced the chance of error through accidental transposition of letters by forming the five letter groups in such a way that in a single series the transposing of two letters does not alter the meaning of the group. Thus, in the series to which HATAN belongs, none of the following groups are included: AHTAN, HTAAN, HAATN, HATNA.

Both numerals and letters may be employed in the formation of codes. But since there are twenty-six letters, as opposed to only ten digits, the number of permutations in five-unit groups is much greater if the alphabet is used. This plenitude is important — although a vocabulary of 10,000 code words can adequately express anything — in view of the fact that word frequency is the vulnerable element in codes as is letter frequency in ciphers. Because of this, many variants for common words must be included in the code, just as in ciphers variants for E, T, and O must be established to increase security. Furthermore, the opportunities for condensing phrases and sentences into five-unit groups should not be neglected. In consequence, secret codes vastly in excess of 100,000 letter groups are not uncommon.

Alphabetical codes are of two general types. The first, which is of very inferior security, is known as a one-part code. Only one half of the bilingual dictionary is necessary for both encoding and decoding. This is because the code groups of letters and their equivalents are arranged in approximate alphabetical sequence. For example:

OPPAL.........OPPORTUNITY (IES)
OPPBM.........OPPOSE (S)

OPPCN.........OPPOSITE
OPPDO.........OPPOSITION (S)
OPPEP.........OPPOSITIVE
OPPFQ.........OPPRESS (ES) (ED) (ING)

The second type is known as the two-part code. It calls to mind the enciphering-deciphering alphabets. One part is used to encode messages, and is so arranged that the words or phrases in plain text are in alphabetical order. In the other part the code equivalents are arranged in alphabetical order for decoding. For example:

| *Encoding* | | *Decoding* | |
|---|---|---|---|
| FLAP | XYMAS | RATPA | SHIP |
| FLAPDOODLE | TIBAL | RATPE | QUITE |
| FLAPJACK | UPTON | RATPI | ENOUGH |
| FLAPPER | UPABS | RATPO | HAPPY |
| FLARE | OHPAP | RATPU | LOXODROMIC |

In code books that are provided with variants to destroy the telltale frequency of common words, a listing somewhat like the following may appear:

ARMY....TORMA, RAFEM, LABAR, ROMUF, IBEXO

Another method for producing variation in the encoded form of a word that must be repeated is to use a syllabary. This is an essential adjunct today to our military and naval code books. To avoid the apparent repetition of a word, a list of syllables is prepared and a code word is assigned to each. If, for instance, in sending a message from a battleship, the word *propeller* must be used a number of times, it may be divided in various ways, and code words substituted for any of the divisions: PRO PEL LER, PROP ELL ER, PROPE EL LER, and so on.

As in ciphers, nulls are used in codes to confound the enemy, and code messages are salted and peppered with meaningless groups of letters.

Since for secret communication in and between our military

services the use of both codes and ciphers is necessary, it may be interesting to compare the merits of the two systems. The summary below is from the point of view of the Signal Corps, U. S. Army.

A message is more rapidly encoded and decoded than it is enciphered and deciphered. The latter method requires much more painstaking care than the former if serious errors are to be avoided, a matter of paramount importance in the combat zone. Although there are mechanical devices that reduce the mental strain when messages are being enciphered and deciphered, and consequently tend to minimize the chances of error, the ciphers formed by them have considerably less security than codes. This is especially true if many messages have been intercepted by the enemy.

However, it should be borne in mind that the security of a given code depends upon its form. It must be a two-part code. The size of its vocabulary, the number of serviceable sentences, and the extensiveness of its variants and syllabaries all affect its security — as does the volume of messages that is to be encoded.

In the case of ciphers, the breaking of a single cipher message discloses the entire system, so that all messages written with the same key can be read by the enemy. This is not necessarily true of a code. However, the printing, distribution, and possession of code books involve dangers, for if the enemy has a chance to see and memorize even a small portion of a code, the whole is compromised.

In time of war, any system, whether code or cipher, must be changed frequently as security at best is of short duration. New ciphers can be substituted at a moment's notice with a minimum of trouble, but to prepare, print, edit, bind, and distribute new code books is a long and arduous task.

If in a transmitted code message one or more groups of letters are obscure, the chances are that the entire message will be meaningless, whereas in a cipher message a few wrong letters may be corrected from the context.

From this comparison it will be seen that the advantages and disadvantages of both systems are numerous. Some of the faults of each can be overcome by combining the two, by enciphering a coded message. And this, quite sensibly, our armed forces have done.

This cursory discussion, brief as it is, gives the salient points both of the similarity and difference between codes and ciphers. Since the breaking of codes is based on a technique that is not very closely related to cryptanalysis of ciphers, we shall omit it altogether rather than risk adding further confusion to a subject that already requires complete concentration for any clear understanding.

# VI

## *Cryptanalysis*

Much has been written about the mental prerequisites for being a cryptanalyst. Certainly the greatest geniuses in this art, as in every other, possess a quality of intellect that defies definition and mystifies more average minds. But though lesser souls cannot hope to equal Beethoven or Michelangelo, they need not, therefore, decline to whistle the latest tune or to touch a pencil. The earnest student is capable of learning the rules and, as an amateur, of enjoying his achievement. Our discussion of cryptanalysis in this volume will attempt no more.

Patience and accuracy are two of the absolute prerequisites. The student will greatly increase his accuracy and efficiency by having at hand sharp pencils of two or more colors, quarter-inch graph paper, a ruler, and above all an eraser. He should confine himself to the use of capital letters, legibly inscribed. Uninspiring though all this may sound, it will obviate many an error, save time, and minimize exasperation.

The first step in attacking any cryptogram is to determine whether it is one of transposition or substitution. This will usually be indicated by the letter frequency. As has already been mentioned, E–T–O–A–N–I–R–S–H are the most recurrent letters in the English language. They should be memorized in that order (see page 153). Pronounce *etoan irsh* and you have it. If the majority of these letters occur very frequently, and their frequency somewhat approaches the order given above, you may be confident that you are dealing with transposition — presuming, of course, that the message is one involving common or garden variety English words. "Zanzibar zany drives zebra zigzag" would not meet the test. In addition to memorizing *etoan irsh*, the student should keep before him a table of common digraphs and trigraphs so that they will soon become familiar (see Appendix D).

Having concluded, let us say, that the message has been enciphered by transposition, the next step is to determine the number of possible geometric patterns into which the letters of the cipher text will exactly fit (see page 37). This number, times the number of possible route inscriptions (see page 41), exhausts the number of ways in which the plain text could be concealed. As the number is enormous, we have in our problems at the end of the volume arbitrarily limited the possibilities, and have indicated the limitation in each case. For example, the direction of the inscription or transcription may be indicated, or one of two optional directions specified. If the problem involves columnar transposition, then the fact that the message has been inscribed horizontally and transcribed vertically may be mentioned. We believe that in spite of this gratuitous information, the transposition problems are of sufficient variety, and the later examples of sufficient complexity to offer a fair trial for the student's ingenuity. And after all, it is his ingenuity and not his patience that should be tried. Professional analysis often requires a staff of highly trained experts all working on the same message to discover its final type.

In shifting the various possible arrangements and alignments, one must keep a keen watch for logical letter sequences as represented by common digraphs and trigraphs. The importance of this alertness becomes very apparent when we consider the deciphering of a message written on a scytale as mentioned on pages 16–7. It will be recalled that this enciphering involved the use of two identical cylindrical staffs. The sender wound a narrow strip of parchment spirally around the cylinder he retained, and then inscribed his message lengthwise so that when the parchment was unwound the true letter sequence was destroyed. Only the person possessing the other cylinder could, by rewinding the strip thereon, restore the proper order.

Now since the staff is truly cylindrical, the interval between each succeeding letter of the plain-text message is constant. First, then, what this interval is must be discovered. To find it, we make an exact copy and cut off three strips of equal length from one end of the ribbon. These we juxtapose, the first against the second, the second against the third. By sliding them up and down, we can eventually discover a position in which a logical letter sequence is formed, or perhaps more than one. We then note the interval between these letters. Suppose the trigraph WIC appears and the interval between each of these letters is seven. Then the seventh letter after C should be H or K, if we are right, or at least some other letter, if there is one, that would make a logical letter sequence in an English word. If it is not, then we must continue our experiment until such a continuous sequence occurs.

It should be noticed that scytale enciphering involves no system that we have not already discussed. It is only that a different mechanical device has been used in inscribing the message horizontally and transcribing it vertically. Likewise, our method of solution is merely a mechanical aid. And the rapidity with which the cryptogram is broken depends to no small extent upon our perception of logical letter groupings.

When, however, the repeated occurrence of low-frequency letters indicates that a message has been written in a substitution cipher, our procedure is totally different from that described above.

We must first make tables of frequency for single letters, digraphs, and trigraphs (see page 153), and then we must not count too strongly upon normal frequency. The laws of probability are exact only from the point of view of infinity. Were this not so, pure substitution enciphering would be useless, and its analysis a tedious matter of arithmetic, rather than a test of one's ingenuity, intelligence, and reasoning power.

Furthermore, the frequency of letters and letter groups varies with conditions and circumstances. Not only is there a pronounced difference of letter frequency even between etymologically allied languages, but letter frequency differs in different types of expression in the same language. A telegram is likely to be condensed, with a saving of pennies and common words. "I shall arrive in Chicago at four tomorrow and am happy to say I have the signed contract with me," becomes ARRIVING CHICAGO FOUR TOMORROW CONTRACT SIGNED.

Again, letter frequency is affected by the extent of the vocabulary of the persons using language. Letter frequency in an average business letter will differ from that in the editorials of the *New York Times*. In poetry, normal frequency is often distorted by alliteration and onomatopoeia. Letter frequency based upon a dictionary would be most misleading. For all these reasons the cryptanalyst, like the physician, must practice art as well as science. The tables given in Appendix D are no Aladdin's lamps to open magically the closed doors of cryptography. They are merely skeleton keys that are in most circumstances worth trying in the lock.

Another important aid in breaking substitution ciphers is derived from the fact that cipher alphabets are usually based on some system or key. This memory aid necessary to the correspondents provides an opportunity for the cryptanalyst. By invariably recording the cipher equivalent beneath the letter it represents in the normal alphabet, the analyst will often detect valuable clues. The key word may be discovered; if it is at the end rather than at the beginning of the normal alphabet, this fact may be observed; or a reversal of the cipher alphabet may become apparent early in the analysis (see page 104).

Suppose that we have reached some such stage as this:

| | | | | | | | | | | | | | | | | | | | | | | | | | | |
|---|---|---|---|---|---|---|---|---|---|---|---|---|---|---|---|---|---|---|---|---|---|---|---|---|---|---|
| Plain: | *A* | *B* | *C* | *D* | *E* | *F* | *G* | *H* | *I* | *J* | *K* | *L* | *M* | *N* | *O* | *P* | *Q* | *R* | *S* | *T* | *U* | *V* | *W* | *X* | *Y* | *Z* |
| Cipher: | | O | | | | A | | | | E | | | | | | N | | | | S | T | U | | | | |

Note the position of STU under *TUV*. The cipher alphabet appears to be running in the normal direction and to be disarranged by a key word. Four letters before the cipher S we find cipher N. Were the cipher alphabet in normal order, cipher N would fall under plain-text *O* — that is, five letters before T, and not under *P*. One letter between N and S has been omitted. We note cipher O, one of the letters normally between N and S, has already been placed under *B*, and conclude that it is part of the key word. The remaining three letters between cipher N and cipher S (that is, PQR) fit very neatly under *QRS*. Had the cipher alphabet been reversed, the fact would have been revealed by the appearance of UTS under *KLM* and the same deduction drawn with respect to RQP, under *NOP*.

This example, in which the cipher alphabet has been based on the key word HOLIDAY, with the remaining letters in normal order, is given only as an indication of how great an aid in breaking a cipher may be the careful tabulation of equivalents under the normal alphabet. The reader will be able to make numerous other deductions by this method as he progresses with substitution problems.

Having in a very general way discussed the theory of cryptanalysis, we shall now apply its principles practically to the solving of a few typical encipherments. Since in some cases the alphabetic method described above is of no help at all, we shall disregard it when attacking our examples of substitution encipherments. No two people will break a cipher in the same way. Each will identify different letters first;

each may draw the same conclusion, but from different sources. What is obvious to one is obscure to the other, and *vice versa.*

In this dissimilarity of intellectual approach to secret writing lies much of the fascination of cryptanalysis. The processes by which we shall break the substitution cryptograms that follow may not be those that you would follow, or even the most effective. They represent only our own mental processes, which are individual at best.

## Cryptanalysis of a Transposition Cipher

We receive the following jumble of letters, and are required to discover their hidden meaning.

```
I I P O   T A I I   S N P E   L E S E   H C D R
H I T N   K R B T   N N E T   C T A G   E S R I
A P I N   E N N I   N E R S   E W I B   A I E E
T P E K   S R S H   H S H R   H L I N   P E T T
L T O D   P L O O   L R Y E   N W L Y
```

A mere glance reveals a host of E's and T's and O's and N's, while letters of low normal frequency appear relegated to their proper and inconspicuous place. We decide instantly that this is a transposition encipherment, not a substitution. But from habit, we check first; for if we make an error at this stage of our analysis, we may waste hours groping blindly along the wrong road.

Even if grudgingly, we let caution prevail and make out a frequency table:

| | | | | | | | |
|---|---|---|---|---|---|---|---|
| A | \|\|\|\| | H | 𝍸 \| | O | \|\|\|\| | W | \|\| |
| B | \|\| | I | 𝍸 𝍸 \| | P | 𝍸 \| | X | |
| C | \|\| | J | | R | 𝍸 \|\| | Y | \|\| |
| D | \|\| | K | \|\| | S | 𝍸 \|\| | Z | |
| E | 𝍸 𝍸 \|\|\| | L | 𝍸 \| | T | 𝍸 \|\|\|\| | | |
| F | | M | | U | | | |
| G | \| | N | 𝍸 𝍸 | V | | | |

Our judgment seems to be confirmed, as ETOANIRSH, our most common letters normally, are predominant in the cryptogram.

Having reconcluded that we have a transposition cipher to deal with, our first step is to count the number of letters. There are 96, indisputably. And what a comfort it is to find anything incontrovertible in cryptography!

The number 96 gives these geometrical patterns: 2 × 48, 3 × 32, 4 × 24, 6 × 16, 8 × 12, 12 × 8, 16 × 6, 24 × 4, 32 × 3, and 48 × 2.

Now we should start with the first form, 2 × 48, and try every possible route to discover the plain-text message. Failing, we should try the next form, 4 × 24, and so on until the right pattern is found, transcribing the letters in the way shown on page 36.

In time we come to the rectangle, 12 × 8, and block in the letters, as shown below:

```
I I P O T A I I S N P E
L E S E H C D R H I T N
K R B T N N E T C T A G
E S R I A P I N E N N I
N E R S E W I B A I E E
T P E K S R S H H S H R
N L I N P E T T L T O D
P L O O L R Y E N W L Y
```

We can discover the hidden message only by trial and error, or what we may prefer to call our ingenuity. We must plod through this alphabetical labyrinth along each of its circuitous routes.

We discover at once that none of the eight most obvious routes has been followed; the message runs in no direction around the perimeter of the pattern. By experimentation and with reference to pages 41–3 for suggestions, we decide to try route E–5 (simple diagonal), reading diagonally up.

Beginning at the top left hand corner, we read I, drop down one row, and progress diagonally upwards, read LI; drop down another row to K and read, in the same direction, KEP. Continuing in this manner, we decipher an epigram of Oscar Wilde: I LIKE PERSONS BETTER THAN I LIKE PRINCIPLES... The reader may continue for himself.

The person who enciphered this cryptogram by transposing the letters filled in the pattern shown on page 37, following the route we have just discovered. He used one null, the last letter Y. The first line reading across the top was IIPOTAIISNPE. Then he broke up each row of twelve letters into groups of four, transcribing it so that the original cryptogram with which we started on page 96 was obtained.

Now, if instead of transcribing the letters from left to right, row by row, into groups of four, he had transcribed them by taking another complicated route such as the one followed when inscribing the message, perhaps starting from another corner, then it would have required a score of assistants to work systematically on the decipherment. The number of possibilities would have been enormously increased, but with methodical experimentation the solution would still be found in a surprisingly short time.

## Cryptanalysis of an Informal Substitution Cipher

In an informal substitution encipherment the letters of the cipher message are not grouped into units of five or into other artificial units. The number of letters, symbols, or numerals in each cipher group remains the same as in the words of the plain text. This, of course, is never done in the encipherment of military or diplomatic messages, for the practice exposes initial letters and word endings and otherwise simplifies analysis. However, the beginning student will find it advantageous to master the cryptanalysis of informal encipherment before undertaking that of formal encipherment. For this reason, the example below is given, as are the groups of informal substitution problems.

PTOBZ QVKNSYG MV GVKQ YEMMYO AVG
BWC AOBM SEX ISOW SO PWOOFOP
SO VWYG CVOP EM MV BWWVG
AODBKPO SO ZWVIP EM MOBPOP

The letter frequency in this cryptogram is found by making the following table:

| | | | |
|---|---|---|---|
| A | III | N | I |
| B | 𝍸 I | O | 𝍸 𝍸 𝍸 |
| C | II | P | IIII III |
| D | I | Q | II |
| E | IIII | R | |
| F | I | S | 𝍸 I |
| G | 𝍸 | T | I |
| H | | U | |
| I | II | V | 𝍸 IIII |
| J | | W | 𝍸 II |
| K | III | X | I |
| L | | Y | IIII |
| M | 𝍸 III | Z | II |

Listing the letters of highest frequency in order of their numerical importance, we have O = 15; V = 9; M = 8; W = 7; S = 6; B = 6; G = 5; E = 4; Y = 4; A = 3; K = 3; C, I, Q, Z = 2; D, F, N, T, X = 1.

It is of course at once obvious that we have a substitution cipher, not a transposition cipher.

We first try substituting *E* for O, the letter of highest frequency in our table. In the event that this later should prove to be wrong, we should try the V or M or P as second choice for *E*. But first *E*:

```
  E                        E
PTOBZ QVKNSYG MV GVKQ YEMMYO AVG

     E         E   E   EE E
BWC AOBM SEX ISOW SO PWOOFOP

 E        E
SO VWYG CVOP EM MV BWWVG

 E    E  E           E  E
AODBKPO SO ZWVIP EM MOBPOP
```

We now look for the weakest spots in the cryptogram. We are apt to find them in the two- and three-letter words.

If O equals *E*, then none of the three-letter groups can be *THE* since none of them contains an O. Passing quickly on to the two-letter words, we see that both MV and EM occur twice, once immediately next to each other, EM MV. This suggests several pairs of two-letter words with one letter in common, not in the same position:

| | | | |
|---|---|---|---|
| *IS, AS,* | or *US* | and | *SO* |
| *AM,* | or *I'M* | and | *MA* |
| *AN,* | or *IN* | and | *NO* |
| *AT,* | or *IT* | and | *TO* |
| *NO, GO,* | or *DO* | and | *OF, ON, OH, OR* |

The possible combinations seem discouragingly numerous; but if we turn to our frequency tables for help we find AT, IT, and TO are all high-frequency two-letter words. Furthermore, we note that T is normally one of the most frequent single letters, and since M is of very high frequency in the table of this cryptogram, we choose to try it first. This obliges us to conclude that *V* is O, since in MV the only possible vowel to follow *T* is *O*.

We must now decide whether we shall try EM as *AT* or *IT*. We select *IT* because we can think of many phrases with the sequence *IT TO*, such as LEAVE IT TO ME; BUY IT TO KEEP, but few with the sequence AT TO.

We now substitute *T* for M, *I* for E, and *O* for V.

```
  E      O        TO  O    ITT  E  O
PTOBZ QVKNSYG MV GVKQ YEMMYO AVG

     E  T    I   E     E    EE E
BWC AOBM SEX ISOW SO PWOOFOP

 E  O     OE IT TO     O
SO VWYG CVOP EM MV BWWVG

 E    E  E    O   IT TE  E
AODBKPO SO ZWVIP EM MOBPOP
```

The cipher group $\overset{ITT\ E}{\text{YEMMYO}}$ immediately appears as a partial test of the substitutions made so far. If we can find no letter that will take the place of Y to form a word, we shall know that one, at least, of our previous substitutions has been wrong. We go through the alphabet and find that *L*, and *L* only, forms a word. We substitute *L* for Y, realizing that this is at best only negative proof, since the Y occurs in only two other cipher groups, — QVKNSYG and VWYG. However, *L* is a possible substitution for Y in both of these.

Continuing with the two-letter groups, we attack $\overset{\ E}{\text{SO}}$, which occurs three times, and recognize several possibilities: *BE*, *HE*, *ME*, *WE*.

Of these we find only two listed among the frequent two-letter words in the proper table. They are *BE* and *HE*. It seems wisest to experiment with them first. Considering the comparative merits of *B* and *H* as a choice, we note that cipher S has a moderately high frequency in our table, and that this is also the case in the normal frequency of *H*, although *B* has a lower frequency. We are also prejudiced in favor of *H* because although $\overset{BE}{\text{ISOW}}$ might be *ABED* or *ABET;* these words are by no means as common as the words we could construct with $\overset{HE}{\text{ISOW}}$: *THEM*, *THEN*, or *WHEN*.

Experimenting, we enscribe *H* over each S in the cryptogram, having, of course, filled in the *L* for Y.

```
  E    O  HL  TO  O   LITTLE  O
PTOBZ QVKNSYG MV GVKQ YEMMYO AVG

     E T HI   HE  HE    EE E
BWC AOBM SEX ISOW SO PWOOFOP

HE O L   OE  IT TO     O
SO VWYG CVOP EM MV BWWVG

 E    E HE   O   IT TE  E
AODBKPO SO ZWVIP EM MOBPOP
```

Next our attention is attracted to the high-frequency cipher letter W, which occurs in double in the cipher group at the end of the third line, $\text{BWW}\overset{O}{\text{V}}\text{G}$. We conclude that W must represent a consonant if our assumption is correct that O is *E* and V is *O*, for here we have $\text{WW}\overset{O}{\text{V}}$, and directly above, $\text{W}\overset{EE}{\text{OO}}$. It is unlikely that three vowels would occur in such positions.

In consequence we turn to the table (page 153) that shows the frequency of double letters. Of the unassigned double consonants listed there, we have *SS*, *MM*, *FF* to choose from. Before attempting a decision we look for other groups in which W occurs. The group $\text{I}\overset{HE}{\text{SO}}\text{W}$ seems to be a good one to test, because it is short and already has two of its letters assigned. *S* makes nonsense; *M* makes possible AHEM; *F* makes CHEF.

In all probability the beginner would leap to a conclusion and insert *M* for W, only to find later that he cannot form a word from $\text{B}\overset{MMO}{\text{WWV}}\text{G}$.

By giving careful consideration to all the cipher groups in which W appears, we decide against both *F* and *M*, realizing that in this case the frequency table of double letters does not apply. We must approach the problem from a different angle. At least we know that we must find a consonant, and so as first choice select the one that has the highest normal frequency, inasmuch as cipher W in our table is recorded seven times. *N* appears to make sense in each of the groups containing W.

```
     E     O   HL   TO   O    LITTLE  O
PTOBZ QVKNSYG MV GVKQ YEMMYO AVG

 N    E T HI   HEN HE  NEE E
BWC AOBM SEX ISOW SO PWOOFOP

HE ONL   OE  IT  TO   NNO
SO VWYG CVOP EM MV BWWVG

  E       E HE  NO   IT  TE   E
AODBKPO SO ZWVIP EM MOBPOP
```

Two cipher groups, $\overset{HEN}{\text{ISOW}}$ and $\overset{ONL}{\text{VWYG}}$, are now complete except for one letter, and in each case only one substitution is possible. In the first, I must be *W*, since *T*, which would make THEN, has already been assigned for M.

$\overset{ONL}{\text{VWYG}}$ obviously suggests ONLY; and the minute we substitute *Y* for G in $\overset{NNOY}{\text{BWWVG}}$, we see that B must represent *A*. Therefore we can put in *W* for I, *Y* for G, and *A* for B,

```
   EA     O   HLY  TO YO    LITTLE  OY
PTOBZ QVKNSYG MV GVKQ YEMMYO AVG

AN    EAT HI  WHEN HE  NEE E
BWC AOBM SEX ISOW SO PWOOFOP

HE ONLY  OE  IT  TO ANNOY
SO VWYG CVOP EM MV BWWVG

 E  A    E HE  NOW  IT  TEA E
AODBKPO SO ZWVIP EM MOBPOP
```

The cipher is now virtually broken. Henceforth we feel sure of clear sailing.

$\overset{AN}{\text{BWC}}$ gives *AND* or *ANT*. We test *D* and *T* in the group $\overset{OE}{\text{CVOP}}$, finding *DOES* and *TOES*. AND and DOES are both more common words than *ANT* and *TOES*. We elect *D* and rejoice that in either case P is *S*.

The group $\overset{OY}{\text{AVG}}$ gives *ROY*, *JOY*, *COY*, *TOY*, and *BOY*. We try each of the initial letters for A in the group $\overset{EAT}{\text{AOBM}}$. *REAT*, *JEAT*, *CEAT*, make no sense. We choose *BOY* and *BEAT*, and note that $\overset{HI}{\text{SEX}}$ is established in the objective $\overset{HIM}{\text{SEX}}$.

We are now ready to substitute *D* for C, *S* for P, *B* for A and *M* for X.

*S EA O HLY TO YO LITTLE BOY*
PTOBZ QVKNSYG MV GVKQ YEMMYO AVG

*AND BEAT HIM WHEN HE SNEE ES*
BWC AOBM SEX I SOW SO PWOOFOP

*HE ONLY DOES IT TO ANNOY*
SO VWYG CVOP EM MV BWWVG

*BE A SE HE NOWS IT TEASES*
AODBKPO SO ZWVIP EM MOBPOP

Regardless of the fact that most readers will have long since completed the decipherment from memory, we continue our reasoning to the bitter end.

The group *YO* / GVKQ is certainly *YOUR*; *NOWS* / ZWVIP, *KNOWS*, and we note that the little boy *SNEEZES*.

Our last three incompleted groups after substituting *U* for K, *R* for Q, *K* for Z, and *Z* for F, are *S EAK* / PTOBZ, *ROU HLY* / QVKNSYG, and *BE AUSE* / AODBKPO.

We hazard a guess that T is *P*, N is *G*, and D is *C*, to complete Lewis Carroll's famous stanza on penology.

If we now write the cipher letters under the plain-text alphabet, we shall see that only four letters are missing: H, J, L, U:

| Plain: | *A* | *B* | *C* | *D* | *E* | *F* | *G* | *H* | *I* | *J* | *K* | *L* | *M* | *N* | *O* | *P* | *Q* | *R* | *S* | *T* | *U* | *V* | *W* | *X* | *Y* | *Z* |
|---|---|---|---|---|---|---|---|---|---|---|---|---|---|---|---|---|---|---|---|---|---|---|---|---|---|---|
| Cipher: | B | A | D | C | O | | N | S | E | | Z | Y | X | W | V | T | R | Q | P | M | | K | I | | G | F |

The sudden appearance of ZYX suggests that at that point in this shuffled alphabet the key ends. We notice from here on the alphabet is written backward, omitting the preceding letters of the key. At once we perceive the key is BAD COUNSEL and are in a position to decipher the enemy's dispatches, whether he confines them to extracts from *Alice in Wonderland* or transmits more sinister messages.

## Cryptanalysis of Formal Substitution Ciphers

```
CKPKH  GVGCK  UGZQA  GCKUG  CLGPQ  FJZIG
PQQAF  QQLHG  FJZEF  QGKEF  CCQAG  LOULJ
QFRGM  OGPQA  FUGZO  SJBQA  GLOTS  MFOKS
JZKOQ  VKIGE  KOGFJ  ZKJGI  XKJGT  OGMQP
LCGJQ  CXQKO  GPQYD
```

The first step in attacking a formal cipher such as that above, regardless of the number of letters in the cipher groups, is to make a letter-frequency table, as was done with the informal cipher (see page 99).

The letters will be found to have the following count, listed in order of their frequency:

|  |  |
|---|---|
| G | 21 |
| Q | 16 |
| K | 12 |
| F, J, and O | 9 |
| C | 8 |
| L, P, and Z | 6 |
| A | 5 |
| U | 4 |
| E, I, M, and S | 3 |
| H, T, V, and X | 2 |
| B, D, R, and Y | 1 |

Next a table of digraphs is made. It must be remembered that the total number of digraphs is made up of both combinations of the letters juxtaposed, reading from left to right. In the first two cipher groups we have not only CK, PK, HG, VG, and CK, but also KP, KH, GV, and GC. For this reason, a common method of determining the frequency of digraphs is to read off the two-letter combinations from the beginning to the end of the message, classifying them while doing so according to the initial letter. However, we recommend the following method, which permits the omission of digraphs occurring but once, and which is less laborious.

Start with the letter of highest frequency, and list all digraphs *beginning* with that letter. Then do the same with the letter of next highest frequency, and so forth. In this case we begin with G and include all but B, D, R, and Y. The work sheet below will demonstrate.

*Digraph Work Sheet*

| | | | | | | | | | | | |
|---|---|---|---|---|---|---|---|---|---|---|---|
| GV | GC | GZ | GP | GF | GK | GL | GM | GE | GI | GT | GJ |
| I | II | II | IIII | II | I | II | II | I | I | I | I |
| QA | QF | QQ | QL | QG | QV | QP | QC | QK | QY | | |
| 𝍸 | II | II | I | I | I | I | I | I | I | | |
| KP | KH | KU | KE | KS | KO | KI | KJ | | | | |
| I | I | II | I | I | III | I | II | | | | |
| FJ | FQ | FC | FR | FU | FO | | | | | | |
| III | II | I | I | I | I | | | | | | |
| JZ | JQ | JB | JG | | | | | | | | |
| IIII | II | I | II | | | | | | | | |
| OU | OG | OS | OT | OK | OQ | | | | | | |
| I | IIII | I | I | I | I | | | | | | |
| CK | CL | CC | CQ | CG | CX | | | | | | |
| III | I | I | I | I | I | | | | | | |
| LG | LH | LO | LJ | LC | | | | | | | |
| I | I | II | I | I | | | | | | | |
| PK | PQ | PL | | | | | | | | | |
| I | IIII | I | | | | | | | | | |
| ZQ | ZI | ZE | ZO | ZK | | | | | | | |
| I | I | I | I | II | | | | | | | |

| | | |
|---|---|---|
| AG | AF | |
| III | II | |
| UG | UL | |
| III | I | |
| EF | EK | |
| II | I | |
| IG | IX | |
| II | I | |
| MO | MF | MQ |
| I | I | I |
| SJ | SM | |
| II | I | |
| HG | | |
| II | | |

*Recapitulation*

QA = 5; GP, JZ, OG, PQ = 4; KO, FJ, CK, AG, UG = 3;
GC, GZ, GF, GL, GM, QF, QQ, KU, KJ,
FQ, JQ, JG, LO, ZK, AF, EF, IG, SJ = 2

Our next step is to make a table of trigraphs. We start with the digraph of highest frequency and list all the three-letter groups beginning with it. We continue with the next most frequent digraph, and so on, omitting all those that occur but once.

*Trigraph Work Sheet*

| QAG | QAF | GPQ | JZI | JZE | JZK | OGP | OGF | OGM | PQF | PQQ |
|---|---|---|---|---|---|---|---|---|---|---|
| III | II | IIII | I | I | II | II | I | I | I | I |

| PQA | PQY | KOQ | KOG | FJZ | CKP | CKU | AGC | AGL | UGZ |
|---|---|---|---|---|---|---|---|---|---|
| I | I | I | II | III | I | II | I | II | II |

| UGC | GCK | GCL | GZQ | GZO | GFJ | GLO | GMO | GMQ |
|---|---|---|---|---|---|---|---|---|
| II | I | I | I | I | II | II | I | I |

| QFJ | QFR | QQA | QQL | KUG | KJG | FQQ | FQG | JQF | JQZ |
|---|---|---|---|---|---|---|---|---|---|
| I | I | I | I | II | II | I | I | I | I |

| JGI | JGT | LOU | LOT | ZKO | ZKJ | AFO | AFU | EFQ | EFC |
|---|---|---|---|---|---|---|---|---|---|
| I | I | I | I | I | I | I | I | I | I |

| IGP | IGE | SJB | SJZ |
|---|---|---|---|
| I | I | I | I |

*Recapitulation*

GPQ = 4; QAG, FJZ = 3;
QAF, JZK, OGP, KOG, CKU, AGL, UGZ, GFJ, GLO, KUG, KJG = 2

It is now advisable to glance through the cryptogram for longer repeated groups, since it is possible that we might detect words. This would prove very helpful in breaking the cipher. CKUG occurs twice, as does also QAGLO. However, although we may suspect these of being complete words, the evidence is not strong enough to convince us.

We now have gathered all the necessary statistics, and are ready to start. Here's the cryptogram again:

| | | | | | |
|---|---|---|---|---|---|
| CKPKH | GVGCK | UGZQA | GCKUG | CLGPQ | FJZIG |
| PQQAF | QQLHG | FJZEF | QGKEF | CCQAG | LOULJ |
| QFRGM | OGPQA | FUGZO | SJBQA | GLOTS | MFOKS |
| JZKOQ | VKIGE | KOGFJ | ZKJGI | XKJGT | OGMQP |
| LCGJQ | CXQKO | GPQYD | | | |

Let us assume that G, the most frequent letter in the table we have just made, is *E*. Mindful that *THE* is our most common trigraph in normal communication (see Appendix D), we look in the code message for a trigraph recurring with G as the final letter. QAG occurs three times, and KOG twice, so we must look further to determine which is most likely to represent *THE*. We know that *T* is a high-frequency letter and we observe that Q occurs 16 times as opposed to K's 12. We add to this the evidence that *H*, being a low-frequency letter, is more likely to be represented by A, occurring 5 times, than by O, occurring 9 times. Reference to our table of digraphs confirms our suspicion that QAG is *THE*. QA appears 5 times against OG's 4, and *TH* is the most common digraph in the table of normal frequency (Appendix D).

Tentatively, we insert *T* for Q, *H* for A, and *E* for G.

```
       E E     E TH  E   E    E T      E
CKPKH  GVGCK  UGZQA  GCKUG  CLGPQ  FJZIG

 TTH   TT  E         TE       THE
PQQAF  QQLHG  FJZEF  QGKEF  CCQAG  LOULJ

T  E    E TH    E       TH  E
QFRGM  OGPQA  FUGZO  SJBQA  GLOTS  MFOKS

    T     E     E       E      E    E T
JZKOQ  VKIGE  KOGFJ  ZKJGI  XKJGT  OGMQP

  E T    T    E T
LCGJQ  CXQKO  GPQYD
```

Our attention now focuses upon the seventh and eighth cipher groups, $\overset{TTH}{\text{PQQAF}}$ $\overset{TT\ \ E}{\text{QQLHG}}$. In this position, F must represent a vowel. Because of its high frequency (9) it is much more likely to be *O* or *A* than *U* or even *I*. By grouping $\overset{TH\ T}{\text{QAFQ}}$ together, *THAT* is immediately suggested. We know that *THA* is a common trigraph, very common, and QAF occurs twice in our table; *THO* does not appear in the normal high-frequency trigraph table. With an unwarranted faith in averages, we write *A* over all nine F's.

```
       E E     E TH  E   E    E T  A   E
CKPKH  GVGCK  UGZQA  GCKUG  CLGPQ  FJZIG

 TTHA  TT  E  A   A  TE  A    THE
PQQAF  QQLHG  FJZEF  QGKEF  CCQAG  LOULJ
```

```
TA E      E TH   A E       TH   E         A   
QFRGM   OGPQA   FUGZO   SJBQA   GLOTS   MFOKS

    T      E      EA       E       E     E T 
JZKOQ   VKIGE   KOGFJ   ZKJGI   XKJGT   OGMQP

  E T     T     E T  
LCGJQ   CXQKO   GPQYD
```

Surveying the result, we find it to be not particularly reassuring. *THAT*, between the seventh and eighth cipher groups, and *THE*, in the eleventh, offer consolation, but not conviction. We consider our latest speculation, *A* for F, once more. *AN* is a high-frequency digraph, *AND* a high-frequency trigraph.

*A* being F, FJ occurring three times, as does FJZ also, *AN*, *AND!* So maybe J is *N* and Z is *D*. We try two more substitutions.

```
        E E      EDTH   E   E     E T   AND E
CKPKH   GVGCK   UGZQA   GCKUG   CLGPQ   FJZIG

 TTHA   TT  E   AND A   TE  A     THE       N
PQQAF   QQLHG   FJZEF   QGKEF   CCQAG   LOULJ

TA E     E TH   A ED     N TH   E         A   
QFRGM   OGPQA   FUGZO   SJBQA   GLOTS   MFOKS

ND  T      E     EAN    D NE      NE     E T 
JZKOQ   VKIGE   KOGFJ   ZKJGI   XKJGT   OGMQP

  ENT     T     E T  
LCGJQ   CXQKO   GPQYD
```

This is more encouraging. We also discover that we have now placed four, *E*, *T*, *A*, *N*, of our five normally most frequent letters, *E*, *T*, *O*, *A*, *N*, and have only the *O* still to find. Since K is our third most frequent letter in the cryptogram, we feel fairly safe in trying *O* for K.

```
O O     E E O    EDTH   E O E     E T   AND E
CKPKH   GVGCK   UGZQA   GCKUG   CLGPQ   FJZIG

 TTHA   TT  E   AND A   TEO A     THE       N
PQQAF   QQLHG   FJZEF   QGKEF   CCQAG   LOULJ

TA E     E TH   A ED     N TH   E        A O 
QFRGM   OGPQA   FUGZO   SJBQA   GLOTS   MFOKS
```

| | | | | | |
|---|---|---|---|---|---|
| *NDO T* | *O E* | *O EAN* | *DONE* | *ONE* | *E T* |
| JZKOQ | VKIGE | KOGFJ | ZKJGI | XKJGT | OGMQP |
| *ENT* | *TO* | *E T* | | | |
| LCGJQ | CXQKO | GPQYD | | | |

A survey of the result gives us pause. We hunt for additional clues. OG occurs four times. We again consult our table of normal frequency. *HE* and *RE* are high in the list. We have already chosen our substitute for *H*. So we essay *R* for O, our decision being bolstered by the fact that *R* is normally very frequent, as is O in the cryptogram.

| | | | | | |
|---|---|---|---|---|---|
| *O O* | *E E O* | *EDTH* | *E O E* | *E T* | *AND E* |
| CKPKH | GVGCK | UGZQA | GCKUG | CLGPQ | FJZIG |
| *TTHA* | *TT E* | *AND A* | *TEO A* | *THE* | *R N* |
| PQQAF | QQLHG | FJZEF | QGKEF | CCQAG | LOULJ |
| *TA E* | *RE TH* | *A EDR* | *N TH* | *E R* | *ARO* |
| QFRGM | OGPQA | FUGZO | SJBQA | GLOTS | MFOKS |
| *NDORT* | *O E* | *OREAN* | *DONE* | *ONE* | *RE T* |
| JZKOQ | VKIGE | KOGFJ | ZKJGI | XKJGT | OGMQP |
| *ENT* | *TOR* | *E T* | | | |
| LCGJQ | CXQKO | GPQYD | | | |

Cipher groups 21, 22, and 23 are now so nearly complete that we can attempt word division. A little study shows that these must be divided as follows: *OREAN DONE ONE* / KOGFJ ZKJGI XKJGT --*AND ONE* --*ONE*. IX must be a two-letter word. We run through the list of two-letter words that would make sense, excluding those which contain letters already assigned. At last we conclude that *BY* is the most plausible substitution, *ONE BY ONE*.

| | | | | | |
|---|---|---|---|---|---|
| *O O* | *E E O* | *EDTH* | *E O E* | *E T* | *ANDBE* |
| CKPKH | GVGCK | UGZQA | GCKUG | CLGPQ | FJZIG |
| *TTHA* | *TT E* | *AND A* | *TEO A* | *THE* | *R N* |
| PQQAF | QQLHG | FJZEF | QGKEF | CCQAG | LOULJ |
| *TA E* | *RE TH* | *A EDR* | *N TH* | *E R* | *ARO* |
| QFRGM | OGPQA | FUGZO | SJBQA | GLOTS | MFOKS |
| *NDORT* | *OBE* | *OREAN* | *DONEB* | *YONE* | *RE T* |
| JZKOQ | VKIGE | KOGFJ | ZKJGI | XKJGT | OGMQP |
| *ENT* | *YTOR* | *E T* | | | |
| LCGJQ | CXQKO | GPQYD | | | |

Of the high-frequency cipher letters all have now been solved but P and L. In the table of normal frequency, all have been placed but *I* and *S*. By substituting *I* for P, we at first think we have been successful because of *ANDBE ITTHA T* / FJZIG PQQAF Q (in the sixth, seventh, and eighth groups), *AND BE IT THAT*, and *TOR EIT* / QKO GPQ, *TORE IT* (in the last two groups). Upon examining *I*'s first appearance (in the first group), however, between two *O*'s *OIO* / CKPKH we suspect defeat. *S* substituted for P is more convincing: *OSO* / CKPKH and *EST ANDBE STTHA T* / CLGPT FJZIG PQQAF Q and *RESTH* / OGPQA and *TOR EST* / QKO GPQ. The result of our substituting *S* for P is as follows:

| | | | | | |
|---|---|---|---|---|---|
| *OSO* | *E E O* | *EDTH* | *E O E* | *EST* | *ANDBE* |
| CKPKH | GVGCK | UGZQA | GCKUG | CLGPQ | FJZIG |
| *STTHA* | *TT E* | *AND A* | *TEO A* | *THE* | *R N* |
| PQQAF | QQLHG | FJZEF | QGKEF | CCQAG | LOULJ' |
| *TA E* | *RESTH* | *A EDR* | *N TH* | *E R* | *ARO* |
| QFRGM | OGPQA | FJGZO | SJBQA | GLOTS | MFOKS |
| *NDORT* | *OBE* | *OREAN* | *DONEB* | *YONE* | *RE TS* |
| JZKOQ | VKIGE | KOGFJ | ZKJGI | XKJGT | OGMQP |
| *ENT* | *YTOR* | *EST* | | | |
| LCGJQ | CXQKO | GPQYD | | | |

Naturally, we now test *I* for L. It gives us *IEST* / LGPQ, *THEIR* / QAGLO, *INTA* / LJ QF, *THEIR* / QAGLO — in every case a natural letter grouping.

Having been piqued by the first cipher group, we now turn our attention to the C, and discover that it appears doubled in the eleventh group. *FF*, *LL*, and *MM* are in the order given, according to our table, the most probable guesses, since *S*, *E*, and *T* have already been established. *F* and *M* give us such impossible combinations as *FOSO* and *MOSO*. *LOSO* at first glance looks as bad, but fortunately it can be broken into *LO! SO* or *LO! SOME*. Testing further, we find it consistently logical, giving *A LLTHE* / F CCQAG, and when we substitute *I* for L, *S ILENTLY* / P LCGJQCX. Besides, *L* as a single letter has a higher frequency than *F* or *M*, and C occurs in the cryptogram 8 times. *L* is our letter.

```
LOSO    E ELO    EDTH    ELO E    LIEST    ANDBE
CKPKH   GVGCK    UGZQA   GCKUG    CLGPQ    FJZIG

STTHA   TTI E    AND A   TEO A    LLTHE    IR IN
PQQAF   QQLHG    FJZEF   QGKEF    CCQAG    LOULJ

TA E    RESTH    A EDR   N TH     EIR      ARO
QFRGM   OGPQA    FUGZO   SJBQA    GLOTS    MFOKS

NDORT   OBE      OREAN   DONEB    YONE     RE TS
JZKOQ   VKIGE    KOGFJ   ZKJGI    XKJGT    OGMQP

ILENT   LYTOR    EST
LCGJQ   CXQKO    GPQYD
```

We now have so many of the letters that the others can easily be solved by trial and error. *V* as U gives *LOVELIEST* (groups 4 and 5) and *HAVE* (groups 14 and 15). *M* as H gives *LO! SOME* (groups 1 and 2) and *TIME* (group 8). *F* as E gives *FATE* (groups 9 and 10), *OF ALL* (groups 10 and 11) and *BEFORE* (groups 20 and 21). Inserting these we have:

```
LOSOM   E ELO    VEDTH   ELOVE    LIEST    ANDBE
CKPKH   GVGCK    UGZQA   GCKUG    CLGPQ    FJZIG

STTHA   TTIME    ANDFA   TEOFA    LLTHE    IRVIN
PQQAF   QQLHG    FJZEF   QGKEF    CCQAG    LOULJ

TA E    RESTH    AVEDR   N TH     EIR      ARO
QFRGM   OGPQA    FUGZO   SJBQA    GLOTS    MFOKS

NDORT   OBEF     OREAN   DONEB    YONE     RE TS
JZKOQ   VKIGE    KOGFJ   ZKJGI    XKJGT    OGMQP

ILENT   LYTOR    EST
LCGJQ   CXQKO    GPQYD
```

Groups 12 and 13, *VINTA E* / ULJOFRG, can only make *VINTAGE*. This is immediately followed by *REST* / MOGPQ, which could be *CREST*, *PREST*, or *WRES1*. Only *PREST*, however, would make sense in this context.

As soon as we have substituted *P* for M in the cipher group 24, *REPT* / T OGMQ, we recognize T as *C*.

| *LOSOM* | *E ELO* | *VEDTH* | *ELOVE* | *LIEST* | *ANDBE* |
|---|---|---|---|---|---|
| CKPKH | GVGCK | UGZQA | GCKUG | CLGPQ | FJZIG |
| *STTHA* | *TTIME* | *ANDFA* | *TEOFA* | *LLTHE* | *IRVIN* |
| PQQAF | QQLHG | FJZEF | QGKEF | CCQAG | LOULJ |
| *TAGEP* | *RESTH* | *AVEDR* | *N TH* | *EIRC* | *PARO* |
| QFRGM | OGPQA | FUGZO | SJBQA | GLOTS | MFOKS |
| *NDORT* | *OBEF* | *OREAN* | *DONEB* | *YONEC* | *REPTS* |
| JZKOQ | VKIGE | KOGFJ | ZKJGI | XKJGT | OGMQP |
| *ILENT* | *LYTOR* | *EST* | | | |
| LCGJQ | CXQKO | GPQYD | | | |

It then becomes obvious that V must be *W*, S must be *U*, and B must be *K*.

> *Lo! some we loved, the loveliest and best*
> *That Time and Fate of all their Vintage prest,*
> *Have drunk their Cup a Round or two before*
> *And one by one crept silently to Rest.*

The key word to the cipher system can now be determined readily enough:

| *A* | *B* | *C* | *D* | *E* | *F* | *G* | *H* | *I* | *J* | *K* | *L* | *M* | *N* | *O* | *P* | *Q* | *R* | *S* | *T* | *U* | *V* | *W* | *X* | *Y* | *Z* |
|---|---|---|---|---|---|---|---|---|---|---|---|---|---|---|---|---|---|---|---|---|---|---|---|---|---|
| F | I | T | Z | G | E | R | A | L | D | B | C | H | J | K | M | N | O | P | Q | S | U | V | W | X | Y |

# VII

## *Problems*

The foregoing discussion of cryptanalysis has, we hope, not only stimulated the reader's desire to try his hand at it, but has also given him sufficient knowledge of its methods to solve the problems that follow. The cryptograms in each group are arranged more or less in the order of ascending difficulty. Our point of view throughout has been at least quasi-professional — that is, our intent has been to present cryptography in its practical aspects. Those who have labored over cryptograms appearing in current publications have often discovered for their pains some such eccentric exposition as

PSORIASIS PESTERS PSITTACINE PARROTS? NOT PTARMIGANS. O PSHAW!

or

JUBILANT JESTER JOYOUSLY JOUNCES JOVIAL JUGGLING JUGGINS.

We have avoided such alliterative jargon altogether, believing that it eschews the very purpose of cryptography, which surely is to conceal what we wish to communicate, not to communicate what is easily concealed. Messages of military or diplomatic import, or even dire secrets of our own, which must be transmitted in cipher are not apt to concern *JUGGINS*, whether jovial or morose, and there is little about a *PTARMIGAN* that could not be mentioned quite openly and candidly.

It should not be inferred from this that the cryptograms that follow contain any messages of great moment, or that their substance recommends them to such obscurity. They are written in a style of literary expression to which we are accustomed, and no attempt has been made either to distort the normal frequency of letters or to preserve it. Furthermore, since there is enough grimness in the texts that the professional cryptographer must decipher, we have refrained from war texts and chosen quotations from literature, noteworthy either for their wisdom or for their utter lack of it.

The general scheme of the section of problems is progressive. The first divisions afford an opportunity to practice regrouping letters visually. The ability to sense logical letter sequences is of great value in all cryptanalysis, and it is especially important in breaking transposition ciphers. In consequence, a beginner will find that he is much more adept at deciphering the more difficult transposition problems if he first practices with the earlier of these enciphements, which have been inscribed without being transcribed. His eye will be quick to detect routes, no matter how devious they may be.

Similarly, in the substitution cryptograms, the beginner will be wise to solve the first and easier problems before attacking the formal encipherments, as he will in so doing have developed a technique that will enable him to make deductions and to find innumerable clues that lack of space has precluded our mentioning. Necessarily our discussion of cryptanalysis was very rudimentary. But having had only the major finger posts pointed out, the reader-cryptanalyst will at least have the thrills of exploration and discovery.

There is a group that contains both substitution and transposition problems, undesignated. However, before attacking it the reader should have developed the ability to detect the difference with ease.

In certain problems, clues are supplied, but they should be used only as a crutch, as a last resort. Correct solutions for all problems are given at the end of the chapter.

## *Group 1 — Perplexing Personalities*

In the following group the unsystematically disarranged letters will, if restored to their proper order, spell the names of well-known people.

1. CLICLURHH
2. PHALOD THIREL
3. CARFON
4. NISLAT
5. KRINNAFL ALENOD OLESERTOV
6. LSMSNIIOU
7. THAMAMA DIGNAH
8. BARLET ININETES
9. CRAINCREBEKK
10. TENGRUHOMA

## *Group 2 — Chaoticgeography*

1. ISURATA
2. NAPDOL
3. CANFER
4. TZARWILDNES
5. TANGEARIN
6. ALIRASUTA
7. IIOAVLB
8. SIGAVOAULY
9. OTLAGRUP
10. UKOHAMUNC

## *Group 3 — Nomina Obscura*

Concealed in each of the following sentences is a name. Its classification is given in italics. In the first sentence is the name of a man, in the second the name of a girl, and so on. The order of the letters spelling each name has not been changed, and there are no intervening letters. You should be able to find them all in six and a half minutes.

1. *A man's name.* As the party meant much to me socially, I kept thinking: Will I amuse my guests more by making them play bridge or charades?

2. *A girl's name.* All Saturday afternoon she made linen pillowslips.

3. *A flower.* While waiting in the garden I attempted to compose myself, for I was nervous and ill at ease.

4. *A country.* A pelican, a dachshund, and a chimpanzee became fast friends.

5. *A city.* The priest pointed out to me that nearly all of the parishioners would contribute to the cause.

6. *A fruit.* When he accused me, neither fear, nor anger, nor pride caused me to betray myself.

7. *A flavor.* Ivan the Terrible! Ivan, ill and dying, was still the terrible.

8. *A vegetable.* A cricket on the hearth heard a wasp in a chimney.

9. *An animal.* One remained in the frying pan, the rest jumped into the fire.

10. *A color.* Although the bull's-eye was large and the target near, only a few hit even the outer circle with their arrows.

## *Group 4 — Literal Litter*

In this group the names of twenty well-known writers have been unsystematically disarranged.

1. OPE
2. ROCAS LIDEW
3. BARNRED WASH
4. RESSKAPEEHA
5. WOLFGONELL
6. CRESAHL SNIDECK
7. RWRWTSHDOO
8. FOGYREEF RECCUHA
9. NNNSTYEO
10. HALPR LADOW REMNOSE
11. DEMNUD NERPESS
12. BRETHER SCNEEPR
13. DYDURAR PILKGIN
14. SELUMA NOSHONJ
15. CRANULEE SNEERT
16. TNSSNVEEO
17. LEGNANOR BRINSWENU
18. YEAKCRATH
19. TAWGHLYORS
20. THAMWET NOLARD

## *Group 5 — Addled Adages*

In the following ten sentences the letters of each word have been disarranged, but the word order has not.

1. SIHT SI ENO EPYT FO ESREVER GNITIRW.

2. HWEN GRYAN, NTCOU NET; ENHW RYEV YRANG, AREWS.

3. OTHNNIG OS SENED REMROFING SA REHOT LEESPOP ITHABS.

4. TI SI TON TEBS TTAH EW DOLSUH LAL KHTNI KIELA; TI SI CEENFIDREF FO NIPOONI HATT SKAME SHORE-ACRES.

5. DAAM DAN VEE DAH NYMA DETSAAVANG, TUB THE CRALPIPIN NEO SAW, TTHA TYEH PEEDCAS GETTNIHE.

6. FI OUY CKIP PU A GRINSVAT GOD NAD KEAM IHM ROOSEPURPS, EH LIWL TON EIBT OUY. HIST SI ETH LAPCIRNIP FREDCENIFE WEBNETE A GOD NAD A ANM.

7. KARMER FO RD. DABLSWIN, NONCENRIGC PUTSRATS: EW TOND REAC OT TEA TOTALSDOSO ATTH HKITN TEHY EAR STRULFEF.

8. GRATININ SI TEYENIVHGR. EHT PHACE SAW CONE A TRIEBT DAMNOL; FROLICALEWU SI HOTGINN TUB BABAGEC WHIT A GELOCEL TUNADOICE.

9. LAMUSE LESCEMN, SHOWE DOESPUNMY SAW KARM INWAT, TOWER DEPHADNUD LISSWON LADERCAN.

10. HATT SI LAL ERETH SI; ETHER STIN NYA ROME.

## *Group 6 — Oscariana*

In the following cryptograms the plain-text message has been inscribed in various systematic routes. There has been no transcription after the inscription.

1.

O E A R S S E E Y H N E C P T M T T O
N C N E I T V R T I G X E T E P A I N

2.

R Y G I H E F U O F A I O M B U H E I N P R T Y E S
C I N S T R E G E P L N W E N T T R U O F E T O N X

3.

L T F L T L S A I A D A R A N G I T U R G A A I T R C I E T I A
X A A Y E U O B S L E T E G D A N H S O E N D S Y I E N S L T L

4.

M O R A O N A F A L I N O T N G C C D S K E C E
E D I T S I T A H T N G I H U S E E I L X E S S

5.

W H E R D O H O H L P I N G A L F R E N S T V E
E V A N A T U G T U H I I S Y S T H L E T I X X
E N A M E S R O Y S D T I T W A O M O B M O S X

6.

```
E T F
M F E
I O I
H H I
T T Y
E S T
I U N
L T U
A C P
```

7.

```
X O D E R T P N A N G B T S H
E F N B A I I E R I E A A I G
N G E E F D H I O N B L T R U
O N T H S N S R F N D L O E A
R I S T I A D F G I A A N T L
```

8.

```
T O D A E T T L A
U A L I S A K N D
B K N N N E B W T
E G O D D E O H H
T T T A I R E I Y
B H B N S W N O S
A O G E O G N O R
U T T R I E N E H
A H L N T L I E T
```

9.

```
W T H N I A W Y E R C
I A E N D H D V E A T
N V G N I O E K N A I
E C A T B N O G T O G
O T E Y A R A U N N C
A T N S B I P F I I Z
I A T K N E O E V I E
E O C A R R B I L D X
```

10.

```
T H E R S I I
O T O C O T T
T T S E N I I
R L E L V S S
E U N F E S S
V C O T R O O
N I F F I D E
O C O T Y S A
```

## *Group 7 — Corinthian Columns*

The messages in the following cryptograms have been concealed by transposition of the columns. After the columns have been restored to their proper order, the texts may easily enough be read from left to right.

1.

```
H T E P
I R M R
S O E P
T A H O
D F A L
I L A N
E C O K
```

2.

```
T W A
S C A
V I A
R E T
O T H
E G E
N E R
A L O
```

3.

```
E B E H T
P R E T T
F O T R A
U O L A V
I D S I R
T E R C S
T Q N O I
```

4.

```
I M S F U
I B T C E
H F O E O
D F O O L
V P A E L
Y N I O G
V M E E E
X E S C S
O I A F T
```

5.

```
O H U T G
H T I H S
M E A B D
S E S N Y
T T H E E
S E M R E
O H D T I
T I A N B
```

6.

```
Y T B I R V E
O S I E S H T
T I U W L F O
```

**7.**

```
W H I E H T
G I G I L R
I M E T F O
N G S I R B
I S R H N I
N G E E V E
```

**8.**

```
N O S T I S F N I
A N T O R M A L O
R A T B O U S I H
A T I V O C Z N O
```

**9.**

```
T I A M L M G O O R
A D V S E I N C O R
P P R E A L Y F F I
A O N R B N U O T M
F M G Y R S A E N L
N T E I V M E A R Y
S P O R F O O V N E
U D S T T O M T A R
S N O O A N T H H I
D O A R M B E O N N
```

**10.**

```
O C E L T I N O N V R G L Y A
N U U O D S O R S O N F E I W
Y T Y O O N N O H E N Y N N N
```

## *Group 8 — Pillars of Hercules*

In the following group the cryptograms have been inscribed from left to right in a rectangular pattern. The columns were then disarranged and the letters transcribed horizontally in arbitrary group lengths.

1. AHLIOTHTEEL BTIEHPSRITI
2. TYMTNA ILADEZ IPSTIR REHLBE DNARYL OPESES
3. PHET STHA LFGO LRYO BADE OTTU GHET EAVR
4. SLAHLAWISNI TGDNIEAPSII DRECEBAESUA MOWAFSNAXRI
5. EACI NEUD NRNO YMWA SEDP TBRI UNTO NARH TOEE OHSP
6. DID IBO UTL ODK ANL AOV EWE HIL TBW ASU RTF OOA NEH LUF HOR
7. ARTIFEA NCHEETM AIENERI RINRTHF EAINNYS KNDZYHA
8. YESRMT AMOISK CLEMAR TKEUYN NGASAN BDESSE MTOMEZ LZVYER
9. EHRSN OIELE OEHEL REVNW BIDRB EFOEE OUNLE IHEWT RSELE IHEEH MSOXZ YREON
10. STDLA NHITL OUHHE TWGIT NOLBI LOTOR ATHMK TTISU KIOVL ONNIA

Here are some clues to certain of the cryptograms (**given in reverse writing**). See p. 131.

4. Ereht si na suoivbo llun gnitacidni eht dne fo eht margotpyrc.
5. Uoy lliw dnif EPOH ta eht dne fo siht.
7. Eht llun lliw evig uoy a DNAH ta eht dne.
8. Owt sllun erew yrassecen ot llif tuo eht htxis wor.
9. Net swor. ON EROM naht eerht sllun.
10. Eht margotpyrc snigeb htiw a noitcnujnoc dna sdne htiw ytilituf.

## *Group 9 — Lost Trails*

In the following group the messages have been transcribed from left to right in arbitrary groupings, having been inscribed in rectangles by various routes.

1. HLDI RGMN FOBH NHFU DTES XIIG EEHS EIET RMEI DEON ILSE CTNX

2. BEUPN ETRAT WHYTM AEOIE RFFEN

3. NTO OAW NOS OSR OWB RHE SSI IAI HWI NRO GFI HGD SHI THS

4. THRD ALAT TPHX FEAW ELOM HRCY IBEE RAGI GEAZ

5. FTAHW ELAME TRAEH OGNAC SIDDL WESIP ACTAH EVAST OTESR JHSIF

6. (a) * XGNI HTEL TNEG ASIR ETSY OEHT
   (b) * XGNISU OYSSEL NUEMOC TNOWTI

7. ADEK REUQ NMAS IHTU HETR TTUB ETIS ILAS HATI WLLA FTER ADNA

8. ACAY RFKV TNEE ADSE ONDB ENRK OOER

9. HEBETSSS SEITISOO ESNFROSA UPLLSIEL

10. WITI NTOM FSTD GATG YOGH LHWO ELRN WETY VBTI IIHL LOUH KHNS ODLT GNTG IHMY LIOW

* The two parts are each to be solved independently.

## *Group 10 — Pot-pourri — Informal Substitution*

THBIP SYAQ QJB
MHB THBIP SYIQI SPIIQ
FAISY SYI OJB —
X JD QJFJGJH KIMQI.
YI'Q HJS AH SYAQ YJFI,
OTS JHFX YAQ KJB,
YI QYIFFIB JTS YAQ QJTF
MHB VIHS TK SJ YAQ LJB.

2. VTGD EWT QJI SWPZ WE LGATOIZ HWJX.
KJW ROIR OX QJI DIGT IOLJQIIX JPXRTIR GXR WXI.
DWP YGD OE DWP VZIGSI, WT ZIQ OQ GZWXI,
EWT OQ OS GZZ WXI QW LGATOIZ HWJX,
KJW ROIR OX QJI DIGT IOLJQIIX JPXRTIR GXR WXI.

3. ZDSO, VDK DM JLO TXR, RLD ZXB JXTN AM VDK ETOXHO,
JATT JLO SXB AB JLO SDDB RATT XTTDR AJ'H X ZLOOHO.

4. N ILDQO VWL ODC D TLWMYLXDW PDC
MIDM SQNXNWDYP HIV DQL SKM NW MHV
SDW IDQOYC ALLY MIL ADMDY PMLLY
DWO PV DQL PYDNW HNMIVKM XKSI UDNW.

5. VYCCYB HROMRT KRRW ST SFB
STM ESIB ZBO URKZBO LROKD GZSAWN;
GZBT NZB NSG GZSK NZB ZSM MRTB,
NZB ESIB ZBO LSKZBO LROKD RTB.

6. UC KNQKN PG KYEZJ YK HNLC WNNQ,
UC KNQKN PG ZNSLYQE FNSW.
PQN JYUN Y KSF S UPIQJSYQ OSKK,
TIJ AYA QPJ ZNSL YJK ONSW.

7. HC XEO A VNJPE PCE "KQNKDE SJV";
A'F OJNNX GJV A VNJPE AP!
YQP A SHG PEDD XJQ HGXCJV,
A'DD BADD XJQ AR XJQ MQJPE AP.

8. XUF XEPPCU VEM E MGCAOUL XGCA
EFA QMUA PG VEL'M ECELDM;
XQP E HEFFGF-XECC PGGB GSS IOM CUTM,
MG IU CEOA AGVF IOM ELDM.

9. PERQXM AJEI KPJ QXCHAQZKQYXC
GZYX KPJ KYWFCKYXJC
YL KPJ MAJEK EXI VQKKVJ HJWJKJAQJC,
OEXM ZJXM EIRQCJI KPJ JWZJAYA
KY TQVV EVV KPJ VQRQXM
EXI AJCGAAJHK KPJ IJEI.

10. KBLVOBZLKABZF ZOYKLOZLKAB CZN YV WVTKBVW ZU LPV UDYULKLDLKAB AT CZBN YDOBKBQ MDVULKABU TAO Z UCADFWVOKBQ ABV.

## *Group 11 — Shakespearean Hours: Informal Substitution*

1. UGPO HN CFSW? 'OHN EFO GWMWPROWM;
JMWNWEO DHMOG GPOG JMWNWEO CPQIGOWM;
UGPO'N OF AFDW HN NOHCC QENQMW;

HE YWCPX OGWMW CHWN EF JCWEOX, —
OGWE AFDW BHNN DW, NUWWO-PEY-OUWEOX,
XFQOG'N P NOQRR UHCC EFO WEYQMW.

2.

JER KIWWRL'K AXPGRL SK JP JER KIWWRL KGRRJ,
JEPIVE JP SJKRXA SJ PQXD XSHR OQB BSR;
UIJ SA JEOJ AXPGRL GSJE UOKR SQARTJSPQ WRRJ,
JER UOKRKJ GRRB PIJULOHRK ESK BSVQSJD:
APL KGRRJRKJ JESQVK JILQ KPILRKJ UD JERSL BRRBK;
XSXSRK JEOJ ARKJRL KWRXX AOL GPLKR JEOQ GRRBK.

3. ENCQ KL JLQN SAN ANCS L' SAN RTK
KLQ SAN ETQBLTR VBKSNQ'R QCYNR;
SALT SAX VLQGMGX SCRF ACRS MLKN,
ALJN CQS YLKN CKM SC'NK SAX VCYNR:
YLGMNK GCMR CKM YBQGR CGG JTRS,
CR IABJKNX-RVNNOR, ILJN SL MTRS.

4.

ELO WS, WCDAC KLW RSCLHI TCSQS MOSQSKT IPYQ,
CPVS SYSQ TL WLKISO, RUT HPAG TLKBUSQ TL MOPDQS.

5.

CJV, QYKS CUCX, QYA TAOX HBOVP COA GSQA:
KO, BL QYAX PBJR, 'QBP UBQY PK VSFF C IYAAO,
QYCQ FACTAP FKKE MCFA, VOACVBJR QYA UBJQAO'P JACO.

6. XKCOO L FRPSCWH ZKHH ZR C XBPPHW'X GCT?
ZKRB CWZ PRWH OREHOT CQG PRWH ZHPSHWCZH.

7.

SAV KREFXDVFZKSR XSQFZKQFX XFVNFX AX YFPP
YJFR SAV EFFT TPSZX ES TBPP, BRE ZJBZ XJSAPE ZFBDJ AX
ZJFVF'X B EKNKRKZO ZJBZ XJBTFX SAV FREX,
VSAIJ-JFY ZJFQ JSY YF YKPP.

8. HPKJ JXPF JXWQU, ITGNFKT JXPF NLJ EWLJFPFK,
JXTLT KXNSS IT QP RPLT GNUTK NQH NST?

9. MRLU MRLC ETP OJGGLU YTC GZG FLLS,
KUG ETP OTPPTF OJUA,
MRKM OJNR K XZUA ORTJWG SWKC IT-SLLS,
KUG AT MRL ETTWO KVTUA.

10.
CHZ, QUUP, ZKG RUXS NS XHYYGZ RBSZQG DQBF,
MBQPY U'GX ZKG FGM UI EUS KNJK GBYZGXS KNQQ.

## *Group 12 — Quid pro Quo: Informal Substitution*

1. D THDON MAAM NDOLEAO LEDU LEA CZDUL HEAU EA EDM LEA CZDUL'M MERKWTAO LR VRKUL RU.

2. LKG SGBPUZG WI B SBV'P QMIG MP LKG AGQQ PXGVFMVJ WI ML BVF VWL LKG QGVJLK.

3. # !#/ #@:#"¢ *%#¢$¢ # :?!#/ –/&,@ ¢%$ *#&*%$¢ %,!.

4.
SAGPG MJGQ SAG KCPQJI, J NFFTQSPNJTQ QKCPD!
CIR SAGPG, QECPEG FGQQ NFFTQSPNJTQ, MJGQ SAG EFGPD.

5. TCHSK ECKJ OHGG JUTBGK NAPB.
VCRB KAUT MTHBSE'J UPDTBGGC IAPB.

6.
42–11 45–13–55–23–31 33–13–14, 45–32–14–42 51
54–11–44–11–43–54–14–13–44–15 14–13–33–11,
51–34–34–11–44–14 14–42–11 33–13–34–11 55–54–13–33 42–32–34
52–51–41–11 42–32–34 13–45–33.

7. KXFMF RFHFM GPL P ZQQI GPM QM P API OFPCF.

8. VIQZ OL OZ, ZITF, ZG IQCT, GK IQCT FG VOYT,
WXZ LOFUST ZIKQSRGD, GK RGXWST LZKOYT?

9. S DSVR SF QUR NLHWO HA BHDDSQY, FHQ PH ETNU QH RFBHY NHEJIFY IP QH PUTF EYPRDA.

10. 56)&- *%2* ¢%6–*&4 2'# %4'- *%2* 3)9¢
¢6&& 2&¢2/- %2¼4 $½' ¢%4)4¼4) *%4/ 59.

## *Group 13 — Subdolous Substituents*

This group consists of formal substitution encipherments.

1. HYGVM HVMLS VKXSO SHPKO SOHMK UIUWD UPKDP
GSVMN HVMDU SNKOS VHYSM SFSPB MHBOS IXHME
OSVOS RJKUV OGNIX UKOSN

2. QAYCY ODNYK BQAYI KQABK NQAYO QPNKB QAYJD SAQBK NQAYI KNNKV QAYCY UKQDK JQKOK IYQAD JSPBP NBNKI QAYOL AYNYK BKTNO KNNKV

3. SFAPA GQLMD MMRGL ZPDTG LDVGS FSFAG LAUGS ZEJAS FAMLJ XZPDT KALSZ UZGJZ EJAVG SFZLA ZQSVG LRGQS MNTSM LXMTP MUAPB MZSAA

4. BFAU UZCU PKVF PBPK RXJL UCTF JLZF BKJB XQZK XUZC BQJC ULJD UUZC PUCB VQJQ ZDUM UZFK UWBJ WZKX UYES

5. BCQAX HJJAC NCBIY XGIAC NGJCW RPIXB KJAIB JACNE NHJYI KXEBI KDIGD IJNXW WUHJX BKHJR WWUCN IPIGW XHJRB MHDAI GIHCT AIXPI BJAXJ JREIE XUZIX HIBVD

6. SLZZK KSERR OPPSL GHITZ YWAGD ZESLG RHPHP RZESL GRHPS GEDES LGRHP ZGYRS LGSPH ZFGHR ZZESL GRHPU ESPYY ZAGYS ZZHPK PPIZK KVWXV

7. VFBLJ MUBJK VMKCL VCLSQ CDCUM TPCLY DGLYQ SMMJC SBSFC SKCLV MLSAB LYVFC SBCPS FJXRG PRTKQ SCLRB RCLQC UBFBP DPMKY GQCNN MGLSK BLSGL SFBBL YSFBM LJXVC XSMAP GLEFG KMUBP SFBJC QSBWN BPGKB LSSMS PXVFB SFBPC FTQAC LYMPC JMUBP GDFBF CUBDB BJGLE GQSMR PXWXZ

8. QBCPN KAFJN IFJFQ YCOPQ UZOZY OCZJN PRSQU BZJFL CMSZR ZAFJQ BZNKA QKAFC JPKIZ LOCXF QZZJN PUZJQ IFNFJ NRCQQ BZIFJ RSQPK KJFUK JNZOE FIZQK HCABQ QBFQP BKUZN QBZOK ASZPQ BZWHC ZNQBZ IFJOZ EKTZO ZNKYQ BZRCQ ZQBZN KACQU FPQBF QNCZN

9. VHYQD APGVA YKHPD KFATK YUAQD HJJQD KOQDJ SNDQQ DVHQJ FJTKV HYEKF JTKYE XGKBC

10. YMOGH KXHNL DHJXM HGHIN MTFNO XWBWG BWLBT KLNCI YOMON DHJXM HBJBR RPACE

## *Group 14 — Gallimaufry*

In the following group some of the messages have been enciphered by substitution, and others by transposition as in group 9.

1. EMJMK LCLEM TEYJN MJUEC KMFRN FAMKU MFJRX MBCUL CLEMN YROUE CEYKB CBMKR JEMJM KLCLE MHRJA URLEY FYRJC SZAPM MWMKY BOEMJ MKLCL EMBWN FEURL EZPLC BMKRJ

2. LEXUA UDMTM FLRST QMOIQ MRRUS NYRRE XMERY CUSLF EXUEL ILVMX YRRXU XMTFL ENUUF TLNUA TYFQU RMTEL QELNU AMFSY SLFEE XYFPE XMEXU UCUAD YRRJK

3. ESRO WLAE DTAE RGAS EMIT EMOS DNAM IHED AMNE VAEH SASI NAMY REVE

4. CSPOE IAONI YUCFE REFSI TENTW ROMEE DAMMO KAORE YRKWM ETEOH HWRET

5. BUUTJ JVTOW KJFAJ GANBA ANJOW KJFAJ GTZIB TBUUU XXRTI JUUXY AXANJ QBPWG OFJGJ IJSIC

6. RHERB OOLEU FHYYT KEBEA OHOSH OTOWS LOKEH ATQRE RDEEG EEDSA VLAEV ENEME

7. RTHSH OANEU NFBIB ITDID SDHNR SLREA OTIIH OLEPB EFWLA HSAHO

8. LOGOH EINVE NAATW FEERI GMFOE DNYSS AORDA ISIIB NLSSO ERSAL DAAHR CIIYG WMWIS NRWNS ANOUV AROAD

9. BUOBP OBPOB VLMUP GSEBL DSKUG BPOBA LTUGB HNOPA UNOHM HKOQG UMHKO BUXPK ULFIU SLFUG ONOHA KUPOU GOUKI KLNUN ULOBU KHMTL KOQUH KFLNE BLUMZ

10. JNIJK JNRFA KRJNQ HKNNR KAWOK RIPNK VWOJF APRVG RQYRK JCVHK NVHYE JNAWZ NRWRG RQPVH YEQRP IUJHQ RJNRS AQKJS AWRPI QRYRK KQIUJ HQRYZ

## *15. The Task of Sisyphus*

UOOGR VURTO NOPTO JCOKY VESUU RLUSU JRHQD AJITI LIUOO GRVUR TMIYR TTTYT MKWMG VGXDJ RHRON OQBMQ BQROC DPELR MQUCG MMUOJ PNCQR MPVBQ DTGNU RHTXV KPNGU OJIKM AWUQB MFNTQ PCQDM GVCGM RLTMY WGGOM HBKJO UIUVC YMRMJ IKMAW ULEKI MNDNY HDJMZ KNGMN IKUDJ MIKGE GLRKN UEIWG HHUQO IJVBQ EKIMH XOYRH QNOCH OQLKY MNKHI VCG

The cryptogram given above presents several perplexing problems. Unless you have considerable skill you will be spared much drudgery by accepting a few hints. These bisques are offered gratis, but they should be taken in the order they are given. If the bisques prove insufficient help, clues may be resorted to. Both bisques and clues are given in reverse writing so that they need not be used if you prefer to rely on your own ability.

*First Bisque:* Fi eht redaer sah ydaerla edam a rettel-ycneuqerf elbat fo siht margotpyrc, eh dluohs eciton taht eht latot ecnerrucco fo M, U, O, R, K, Q, G, N, dna I si eno derdnuh dna ytrof-owt tuo fo owt derdnuh dna ythgie-thgie srettel ni eht egassem. Siht si ylraelc a noitutitsbus tnemrehpicne. Revoerom, ti si tnerappa taht emos fo eseht rehpic srettel tsum evah erom naht eno nialp-txet tnelaviuqe, ecnis revo flah eht egassem si desopmoc fo ylno thgie slobmys. Ni rehto sdrow, ew era gnilaed htiw a citebahplaylop tnemrehpicne.

*Clue 1:* Eton eht ecnerrucer fo UOO ni eht tsrif dna htnin rehpic spourg: fo CGM ni eht htneetenin-hteitnewt dna ni eht hteitriht spourg; fo JIK ni eht ytnewt-htxis dna ni eht ytriht-htfif dna ytriht-htxis spourg.

*Clue 2:* Tnuoc eht rebmun fo srettel neewteb hcae fo eht detaeper shpargirt. Woh ynam srettel era ereht neewteb eht tsrif UOO dna eht dnoces? Dda eerht (eht rebmun fo srettel ni eht hpargirt) rof eht tcerroc lavretni. Tahw si eht elpitlum nommoc ot eht eerht srebmun gnitoned eht slavretni?

*Second Bisque:* Yb gnibircsnart eht rehpic srettel ni eerht snmuloc (sa no egap 73) eht eerht stebahpla lliw eb yltneinevnoc detagerges. A ycneuqerf elbat dluohs won eb edam, tub od ton ekam selbat fo shpargid ro shpargirt tey.

*Public Notice:* Having proceeded this far in the analysis, the reader may turn to page 130, where he will find, for his convenience, a work sheet on which the cryptogram is rewritten in groups that will assist him in keeping the alphabets distinct when filling in his plain-text equivalents.

*Clue 3:* Eht rettel fo tsehgih ycneuqerf ni hcae tebahpla si E, eht txen tsehgih, T.

*Third Bisque:* Shpargid dna shpargirt era tnacifingis ni citebahplaylop smargotpyrc ylno nehw yeht raeppa ni eht emas stebahpla dna ni eht emas evitaler snoitisop — taht si, ni eht emas snmuloc sa degnarra.

*Clue 4:* No eht krow teehs, eton eht tsrif dna htneetfif rehpic spuorg, UOO. O ni eht dnoces tebahpla, esuaceb fo sti noitisop, dluow yllacigol tseggus a lewov ro *H* ro *R* ro *W*. UO, stebahpla eno dna owt, si a detaeper hpargid, dna dewollof yb O ni eht driht tebahpla, si a detaeper hpargirt. Eseht stcaf lliw ediug eht redaer ni gnitceles eht reporp noitutitsbus.

*Fourth Bisque:* Nailp-txet *E* (rehpic M), ni eht htneethgie puorg, sdnats enola sa a elgnis drow.

*Fifth Bisque:* Etirw eht Hsilgne tebahpla no ruoy krow teehs dna tup eht eerht rehpic setutitsbus rednu rieht reporp stnelaviuqe sa uoy dnif meht. Eb erus ot peek hcae rehpic tebahpla tcnitsid.

*Clue 5:* Eton eht dnoces rehpic tebahpla Q srucco ruof semit dewollof yb driht rehpic tebahpla B. Tlusnoc eht elbat rof a hpargid fo hgih ycneuqerf, eht tsrif rettel fo hcihw si *T*.

*Clue 6:* Eht elur fo lamron ycneuqerf seilppa ot eht eerht tsom tneuqerf srettel ni lla eerht rehpic stebahpla.

*Clue 7:* Redisnoc eht tsrif eerht (work sheet) spuorg dna rieht noitideper ni eht htneetfif, htneetxis, dna htneetneves. Ylerus ereh ew evah owt sdrow: *THE* dna B–F–G–L–P–W, *ETTER*. Ecnis G ni eht tsrif rehpic tebahpla srucco neves semit, ti stneserper a rettel fo ylbanosaer hgih ycneuqerf.

*Clue 8:* Eton spuorg ytnewt-xis ot ytnewt-thgie. Eht tnelaviuqe fo Q ni eht tsrif tebahpla si ylriaf tnedive.

*Clue 9:* Ew evah enin s'J ni eht tsrif rehpic tebahpla, ylerus a tol, ecnis siht sesirpmoc ylno eno driht fo eht srettel fo eht margotpyrc. Ti ylbaborp neht stneserper *A* ro *N*. Eton eht nialp-txet srettel ydaerla derehpiced hcihw raeppa no rehtie edis fo eht s'J ni eht tsrif rehpic. Yeht era lla slewov; tahw elbanosaer noisulcnoc od uoy hcaer?

*Clue 10:* Won tup rettel G, eht tsom tneuqerf gniniamer rettel, ot eht emas tset. Hcihw smees eht erom elbaborp, *A* ro *N*?

*Sixth Bisque:* Noituac! Ni eht driht rehpic tebahpla evif srettel era llits deit rof htruof ecalp.

*Clue 11:* Ni eulc 9 ew esohc *N* rof tsrif tebahpla J ni ecnereferp ot *A*. Fi eht wal fo ytilibaborp sdloh eurt, eht txen tsom tneuqerf rettel lliw tneserper *A*. Yrt ti.

*Clue 12:* Tahw ew dias ni eulc 11 tuoba eht tsrif tebahpla yam eb eurt ni eht dnoces tebahpla.

*Clue 13:* Ew evah ruo tsom nommoc hpargirt *THE* ni owt fo sti elbissop stnemrehpicne. Eton spuorg eno (UOO), spuorg ytnewt-xis dna ytnewt-neves. Tub evah ew ton detcelgen ruo txen tsom nommoc hpargirt?

*Clue 14:* Ni eht tsrif tebahpla, gnidrocca ot eht ycneuqerf fo eht dengissanu srettel, T dluohs eb *I* ro *S*. Eton spuorg ytriht-thgie dna ytriht-enin. Nialp-txet *N* (rehpic G) smees ot eb eht gninnigeb fo a drow. Eht gnidecerp rehpic T thgim eb a rettel netfo dnuof ta eht dne fo sdrow.

*Seventh Bisque*: Ebyam uoy evah ot eb ylevitalrepus revelc ot sseug tahw F stneserper ni puorg ytrof-xis; ebyam ton.

*Clue 15:* Rettel ycneuqerf setacidni taht dnoces-tebahpla N dluohs tneserper *I* ro *R*. Fi *I*, ew evah *IE* eciwt, *OI* eciwt, dna *EI* ecno; fi *R*, ew evah *RE* eciwt, *OR* eciwt, dna *ER*.

*Eighth Bisque:* Siht sah neeb derehpicne htiw a Erènegiv elbat; ees egap 71.

*Clue 16:* Eht dnoces tebahpla si owt secalp ot eht thgir fo eht tsrif; eht driht si eerht secalp ot eht tfel fo eht dnoces, ro eno ot eht tfel fo eht tsrif.

## WORK SHEET

UOO GRV URT ONO PTO JCO KYV ESU URL USU JRH QDA JIT ILI UOO

GRV URT MIY RTT TYT MKW MGV GXD JRH RON OQB MQB QRO CDP

ELR MQU CGM MUO JPN CQR MPV BQD TGN URH TXV KPN GUO JIK

MAW UQB MFN TQP CQD MGV CGM RLT MYW GGO MHB KJO UIU VCY

MRM JIK MAW ULE KIM NDN YHD JMZ KNG MNI KUD JMI KGE GLR

KNU EIW GHH UQO IJV BQE KIM HXO YRH QNO CHO QLK YMN

KHI VCG

# VIII

## *Solutions*

The solutions of all the cryptograms are given in reverse writing (that is, each successive word is written backwards) so that the reader will not inadvertently read one until he wishes to do so.

### *Group 1*

1. Llihcruhc. 2. Hploda Reltih. 3. Ocnarf. 4. Nilats. 5. Nilknarf Onaled Tlevesoor. 6. Inilossum. 7. Amtaham Ihdnag. 8. Trebla Nietsnie. 9. Rekcabnekcir. 10. Uahtnegrom.

### *Group 2*

1. Airtsua.
2. Dnalop.
3. Ecnarf.
4. Dnalreztiws.
5. Anitnegra.
6. Ailartsua.
7. Aivilob.
8. Aivalsoguy.
9. Lagutrop.
10. Oukuhcnam.

### *Group 3*

1. Mailliw.
2. Eniledam.

3. Ainedrag.
4. Adanac.
5. Sirap.
6. Egnaro.
7. Allinav.
8. Hcanips.
9. Rehtnap.
10. Etihw.

*Group 4*

1. Eop.
2. Racso Edliw.
3. Dranreb Wahs.
4. Eraepsekahs.
5. Wollefgnol.
6. Selrahc Snekcid.
7. Htrowsdrow.
8. Yerffoeg Recuahc.
9. Nosynnet.
10. Hplar Odlaw Nosreme.
11. Dnumde Resneps.
12. Trebreh Recneps.
13. Draydur Gnilpik.
14. Leumas Nosnhoj.
15. Ecnerual Enrets.
16. Nosnevets.
17. Nonregla Enrubniws.
18. Yarekcaht.
19. Yhtrowslag.
20. Wehttam Dlonra.

*Group 5*

1. Siht si eno epyt fo esrever gnitirw.
2. Nehw yrgna, tnuoc net; nehw yrev yrgna, raews.[1]

[1] Snoitatouq 2–8 morf *Daehn'ddup Nosliw.*

3. Gnihton os sdeen gnimrofer sa rehto s'elpoep stibah.

4. Ti si ton tseb taht ew dluohs lla kniht ekila; ti si ecnereffid fo noinipo taht sekam esroh-secar.

5. Mada dna Eve dah ynam segatnavda, tub eht lapicnirp eno saw taht yeht depacse gnihteet.

6. Fi uoy kcip pu a gnivrats god dna ekam mih suorepsorp, eh lliw ton etib uoy. Siht si eht lapicnirp ecnereffid neewteb a god dna a nam.

7. Kramer fo Rd. s'Niwdlab, gninrecnoc stratspu: Ew t'nod erac ot tae slootsdaot taht kniht yeht era selffurt.

8. Gniniart si gnihtyreve. Eht hcaep saw ecno a rettib dnomla; rewolfiluac si gnihton tub egabbac htiw a egelloc noitacude.

9. Leumas Snemelc, esohw mynoduesp saw Kram Niawt, etorw *Daeh'nddup s'Nosliw Radnelac.*

10. Taht si lla ereht si, ereht t'nsi yna erom.

## *Group 6*

1. Eno nac tsiser gnihtyreve tpecxe noitatpmet.

2. Gniyrc si eht egufer fo nialp nemow, tub eht niur fo ytterp seno.

3. A elttil ytirecnis si a suoregnad gniht, dna a taerg laed si yletulosba lataf.

4. Noitaredom si a talaf gniht. Gnihton sdeeccus ekil ssecxe.

5. Revenehw a nam seod a ylhguoroht diputs gniht ti si syawla morf eht tselbon sevitom.

6. Ytilautcnup si eht feiht fo emit.

7. Rethgual si ton ta lla a dab gninnigeb rof a pihsdneirf, dna ti si raf eht tseb gnidne rof eno.

8. Ereht si ylno eno gniht ni eht dlrow esrow naht gnieb deklat tuoba, dna s'taht ton gnieb deklat tuoba.

9. Htiw na gnineve taoc dna a etihw eit, ydobyna, neve a rekorbkcots, nac niag a noitatuper rof gnieb dezilivic.

10. Ti si os ysae ot trevnoc srehto. Ti si os tluciffid ot trevnoc fleseno.

### *Group 7*

1. Columnar order: 2, 1, 3, 4.

Eht esormirp htap fo ecnaillad.

(Nulls O, K) — *Macbeth*

2. Columnar order: 1, 2, 3.

Sawt' eraivac ot eht lareneg.

(Null O) — *Hamlet*

3. Columnar order: 5, 4, 3, 2, 1.

Eht retteb trap fo ruolav si noitercsid.

(Nulls Q, T) — *Henry IV, Pt. I*

4. Columnar order: 1, 3, 5, 2, 4.

Fi cisum eb eht doof fo evol, yalp no; evig em ssecxe fo ti. (Null A) — *Twelfth Night*

5. Columnar order: 3, 2, 4, 1, 5.

Hguoht siht eb ssendam tey s'ereht dohtem ni ti.

(Nulls A, B) — *Hamlet*

6. Columnar order: 7, 6, 1, 5, 2, 4, 3.

Ytiverb si eht luos fo tiw.

— *Hamlet*

7. Columnar order: 4, 5, 6, 3, 2, 1.

Eht gigilrihw fo emit sgnirb ni sih egnever.

— *Twelfth Night*

8. Columnar order: 4, 5, 6, 1, 2, 3, 9, 8, 7.

Sit' on nis rof nam ot ruobal ta sih noitacov.

(Null z) — *Henry IV, Pt. I*

9. Columnar order: 6, 1, 7, 2, 8, 3, 9, 4, 10, 5.

Latrommi sdog, I evarc on flep;
I yarp rof on nam tub flesym:
Tnarg I yam reven evorp os dnof,
Ot tsurt nam no sih htao ro dnob. Nema.

— *Timon of Athens*

10. Columnar order: 15, 1, 5, 12, 7, 8, 9, 2, 3, 4, 6, 10, 13, 14, 11.

Gnitrevnoc lla ruoy sdnuos fo eow
Otni Yeh ynnon, ynnon.

— *Much Ado About Nothing*

## *Group 8*

1. 11 × 2, key word TO.

Liah ot eeht, ehtilb tirips. — *Shelley*

2. 12 × 3, key word POE.

Ym dezilatnat tirips
Ereh yldnalb sesoper. — *Poe*

3. 4 × 8, key number 4231.

Eht shtap fo yrolg dael tub ot eht evarg.

— *Gray*

4. 4 × 11, key number 1432.

Llahs I, gnitsaw ni riapsed,
Eid esuaceb a s'namow riaf?

(Null x) — *Wither*

5. 5 × 8, key number 43251.

I nac erudne ym nwo riapsed
Tub ton s'rehtona epoh. — *Walsh*

6. 5 × 9, key word *OTWAY*.

    I did tub kool dna evol elihwa,
    Sawt' tub rof eno flah-ruoh. — *Otway*

7. 6 × 7, key number 456123.

    I raef eeht, tneicna Reniram!
    I raef yht ynniks dnah!

    (Null z) — *Coleridge*

8. 8 × 6, key number 51873624.

    Ym retsam semoc ekil yna Krut
    Dna sgnab em tsom ylereves.

    (Nulls z, z) — *Carey*

9. 10 × 6, key word *EXHAUSTION*.

    Ereh seil eno ohw reven deil erofeb,
    Tub won eh seil ereh, eh seil on erom.

    (Nulls x, y, z) — *Anon.*

10. 10 × 5, key number 5 6 3 1 2 8 4 10 9 7

    Dna llits eht thguoht I lliw ton koorb,
    Taht I tsum kool ni niav. — *Wolfe*

## *Group 9*

1. 24 × 2, B–1.[1]

    Eh del sih tnemiger morf dniheb,
    (Eh dnuof ti ssel gniticxe.)

    (Null x) — *W. S. Gilbert*

2. 5 × 5, B–1.

    Eraweb eht yruf fo tneitap nem.
    — [Mis]quoted from *Dryden*

3. 7 × 6, D–1.

On drib sraos oot hgih fi eh sraos htiw sih nwo sgniw.
— *Blake*

[1] This is a reference to the routing table on pages 41–43.

4. 12 × 3, D–3.

Fi eht draeb erew lla, a taog thgim hcaerp.

(Nulls X, Y, Z) — *Old Danish Proverb*

5. 5 × 10, A–2.

Tahw elamef traeh nac dlog esipsed?
Tahw s'tac esreva ot hsif?

(Null J) — *Gray*

6. 8 × 3, A–4.

(a): Eht retsyo si a eltneg gniht.
(b): Ti t'now emoc sselnu uoy gnis.

(Null X in both) — *Anon.*

7. 4 × 12, C–4.

Dna, retfa lla, tahw si a eil? Sit' tub eht hturt ni edareuqsam.

(Null K) — *Byron*

8. 4 × 7, E–1.

A ytfarc evank seod deen on rekorb.

— *Shakespeare*

9. 4 × 8, G–4.

Erusiel si eht tseb fo lla snoissessop.

— *Socrates*

10. 8 × 8, F–7.

I dloh ym evol tub ylthgil rof I wonk
Sgniht htiw sgniw dleh ylthgit tnaw ot og.

(Null M) — *Jewell B. Tull*

## *Group 10*

1. Key: *MORBIDLY*, at beginning of alphabet, remaining letters in normal sequence.

Rednu siht dos
Dna rednu eseht seert

Hteil eht dob-
y fo Nomolos Esaep.
S'eh ton ni siht eloh,
Tub ylno sih dop,
Eh dellehs tuo sih luos
Dna tnew pu ot sih dog.

— *From an Ohio tombstone*

2. Key: *GABRIEL JOHN*, at beginning, remaining letters reversed.

Yarp rof eht luos fo Leirbag Nhoj,
Ohw deid ni eht raey neethgie derdnuh dna eno.
Uoy yam fi uoy esaelp, ro tel ti enola,
Rof ti si lla eno ot Leirbag Nhoj,
Ohw deid ni eht raey neethgie derdnuh dna eno.

— *Anon.*

3. Key: *COMPLAINTS*, after *XYZ*, remaining letters following in normal sequence.

Emoc, uoy fo eht wal, ohw nac klat fi uoy esaelp,
Llit eht nam ni eht noom lliw wolla s'ti a eseehc.

— *O. W. Holmes*

4. Key: *DESOLATING*, at beginning, remaining letters in reverse sequence.

I draeh eno yad a nameltneg yas
Taht slanimirc ohw era tuc ni owt
Nac yldrah leef eht lataf leets
Dna os era nials touhtiw hcum niap.

— *W. S. Gilbert*

5. Key: *SHAMBLE*, at beginning, remaining letters reversed.

Eizzil Nodrob koot na exa
Dna evag reh rehtom ytrof skcahw;
Nehw ehs was tahw ehs dah enod,
Ehs evag reh rehtaf ytrof-eno. — *Anon.*

6. Key: *STRANGE*, at beginning, remaining letters reversed.

Ym esnes fo thgis si yrev neek,
Ym esnes fo gniraeh kaew.
Eno emit I was a niatnuom ssap
Tub did ton raeh sti kaep. — *Oliver Herford*

7. Key: *HYSTERICAL*, at beginning, remaining letters in normal sequence.

Ha Sey I Etorw eht 'Elprup Woc';
M'I Yrros, won, I Etorw ti!
Tub I nac Llet Uoy Wohyna,
Ll'I Llik uoy fi uoy Etouq ti.

— *Gelett Burgess*

8. Key: *EXHAUSTION*, at beginning, remaining letters in normal sequence.

Neb Elttab saw a reidlos dlob
Dna desu ot s'raw smrala;
Tub a nonnac-llab koot ffo sih sgel,
Os eh dial nwod sih smra. — *Thomas Hood*

9. Key: *BACKGROUND*, at end, remaining letters in normal sequence.

Gnivah daer eht snoitpircsni
Nopu eht senotsbmot
Fo eht taerg dna elttil seiretemec,
Gnaw Gnep desivda eht Rorepme
Ot llik lla eht gnivil
Dna tcerruser eht daed. — *Paul Eldridge*

10. Key: *SMOULDERING*, at end, remaining letters in reverse sequence.

Lanoitanretni Noitartibra yam eb denifed
sa eht noitutitsbus fo ynam gninrub snoitseuq
rof a gniredluoms eno. — *Ambrose Bierce*

### *Group II*

1. Key: PLAYWRIGHT, at beginning, remaining letters in normal sequence.

Tahw si evol? Sit' ton retfaereh;
Tneserp htrim htah tneserp rethgual;
S'tahw ot emoc si llits erusnu:
Ni yaled ereht seil on ytnelp, —
Neht emoc ssik em, Teews-dna-ytnewt,
Shtuoy a ffuts lliw ton erudne.

— *Twelfth Night*

2. Key: OUTBRAVES, at beginning, remaining letters in reverse sequence.

Eht s'remmus rewolf si ot eht remmus teews,
Hguoht ot flesti ti ylno evil dna eid;
Tub fi taht rewolf htiw esab noitcefni teem,
Eht tsesab deew sevarbtuo sih ytingid:
Rof tseteews sgniht nrut tseruos yb rieht sdeed;
Seilil taht retsef llems raf esrow naht sdeew.

— *Sonnet* xciv

3. Key: CHIMNEY, at beginning, remaining letters in normal sequence.

Raef on erom eht taeh 'o eht nus
Ron eht suoiruf s'retniw segar:
Uoht yht yldlrow ksat tsah enod,
Emoh tra enog dna ne'at yht segaw:
Nedlog sdal dna slrig lla tsum,
Sa yenmihc-speews, emoc ot tsud. — *Cymbeline*

4. Key: PRAISE, at beginning, remaining letters in normal sequence.

Rof ew, hcihw won dloheb eseht tneserp syad,
Evah seye ot rednow, tub kcal seugnot ot esiarp.

— *Sonnet* cvi

5. Key: *CHIVALRY*, at beginning, remaining letters in normal sequence.

Dna, uoht yawa, eht yrev sdrib era etum:
Ro, fi yeht gnis, sit' htiw os llud a reehc,
Taht sevael kool elap, gnidaerd eht s'retniw raen.
— *Sonnet* xcvii

6. Key: *BEAUTY*, at end, remaining letters in normal sequence.

Llahs I erapmoc eeht ot a s'remmus yad?
Uoht tra erom ylevol dna erom etarepmet.
— *Sonnet* xviii

7. Key: *ANYHOW*, at end, remaining letters in normal sequence.

Ruo noitercsedni semitemos sevres su llew
Nehw ruo peed stolp od llap, dna taht dluohs
hcaet su
S'ereht a ytinivid taht sepahs ruo sdne,
Hguor-weh meht woh ew lliw. — *Hamlet*

8. Key: *NIGHT*, at beginning, remaining letters in reverse sequence.

Tsod uoht kniht, esuaceb uoht tra suoutriv,
Ereht llahs eb on erom sekac dna ela?
— *Twelfth Night*

9. Key: *KING LEAR*, at beginning, remaining letters in reverse order.

Neht yeht rof neddus yoj did peew,
Dna rof worros gnus,
Taht hcus a gnik dluohs yalp ob-peep,
Dna og eht sloof gnoma. — *King Lear*

10. Key: *HAMLET*, at end, remaining letters in normal sequence.

Tub, kool, eht nrom ni tessur eltnam dalc,
Sklaw re'o eht wed fo noy hgih nretsae llih. — *Hamlet*

### *Group 12*

1. Key: *DISTANCE*, at beginning, remaining letters in reverse order.

A frawd sees rehtraf naht eht tnaig nehw eh sah eht s'tnaig redluohs ot tnuom no. — *Coleridge*

2. Key: *PLUTARCH*, at end, remaining letters in normal sequence.

Eht erusaem fo a s'nam efil si eht llew gnidneps fo ti dna ton eht htgnel. — *Plutarch*

3. Signs picked arbitrarily as follows:

| | | | | | | | | | | | | | | |
|---|---|---|---|---|---|---|---|---|---|---|---|---|---|---|
| Cipher: | # | * | $ | % | , | @ | ! | / | ? | ¢ | & | - | : | " |
| Plain-text: | A | C | E | H | I | L | M | N | O | S | T | U | W | Y |

A nam syawla sesahc a namow litnu ehs sehctac mih.

— *Unknown*

4. Key: *CLERGYMAN*, at beginning, remaining letters in normal sequence.

Ereht seog eht nosrap, O suoirtsulli kraps!
Dna ereht, ecracs ssel suoirtsulli, seog eht krelc.

— *Cowper*

5. Key: *SECURITY*, remaining letters inscribed horizontally beneath it and transcribed vertically in the numerical order of the letters in the key word — C 1, E 2, I 3, et cetera, for cipher alphabet (see page 64).

Yniar syad lliw ylerus emoc.
Ekat ruoy s'dneirf allerbmu emoh. — *Unknown*

6. Key: 52431, under which the alphabet is blocked; then the cipher numbers are taken from the numerical key and the row numbers (see page 65).

Eh dluow ton, htiw a yrotpmerep enot,
Tressa eht eson nopu sih ecaf sih nwo.

— *Cowper*

7. Key: *PACIFY*, at beginning, remaining letters in reverse order.

Ereht reven saw a doog raw ro a dab ecaep. — *Franklin*

8. Cipher alphabet taken from order of letters on standard typewriter keyboard.

Tahw si ti, neht, ot evah, ro evah on efiw,
Tub elgnis modlarht, ro elbuod efirts. — *Bacon*

9. Key: *IGNORAMUS*, at beginning, remaining letters in normal sequence.

I evil ni eht dworc fo ytilloj, ton os hcum ot yojne ynapmoc sa ot nuhs flesym. — *Johnson*

10. Cipher taken from normal position, then shift, of each successive key of top row of standard typewriter, and then last keys of each row, thus

2"3#4$5%6_7&8'9(0)-*½¼¢@/?

Slrig taht eltsihw dna sneh taht worc
Lliw syawla evah nuf reverehw yeht og.

— *Anon.*

## *Group 13*

1. Key: *GOLDSMITH*, in reverse writing at beginning of alphabet, remaining letters in reverse order.

A dnik dna eltneg traeh eh dah,
Ot trofmoc sdneirf dna seof;
Eht dekan yreve yad eh dalc
Nehw eh tup no sih sehtolc. — *Goldsmith*

2. Key: *PERCYBS*, at beginning, remaining letters in normal order.

Eht erised fo eht htom rof eht rats,
Fo eht thgin rof eht worrom,
Eht noitoved ot gnihtemos rafa,
Morf eht erehps fo ruo worros. — *Shelley*

3. Key: *ZEBRA*, at beginning, remaining letters in normal order.

Ereht si on doog ni gniugra htiw eht elbativeni. Eht ylno tnemugra elbaliava htiw na tsae dniw si ot tup no ruoy taocrevo.

(Null A) — *Lowell*

4. Key: *ADVISE*, at end, remaining letters in reverse order.

Eurt esae ni gnitirw semoc morf tra ton ecnahc;
Sa esoht evom tseisae ohw evah denrael ot ecnad.

(Nulls Y, E, S) — *Pope*

5. Key: *XYZKITMARLOWE*, remaining letters in normal order.

Won tsah uoht eno erab ruoh ot evil
Dna neht uoht tsum eb denmad yllauteprep.
Dnats llits, uoy gnitsalreve serehps fo Nevaeh,
Taht emit yam esaec. (Nulls B, V, D) — *Marlowe*

6. Key: *REPUBLICAN*, at beginning of plain-text alphabet, remaining letters in normal order, enciphering alphabet beneath it beginning *YZABC*, and so on.

Eht gge sit' htooms dna yrev elap,
Ti sah on eson, ti sah on liat:
Ti sah on srae taht eno nac ees,
Ti sah on tiw ro eetraper, —
On doog gge. (Nulls Y, W, X, V) — *Bishop*

7. Key: *CARY*, at beginning, remaining letters in normal order.

Nehw ylevol namow stnaw a ruovaf,
Dna sdnif oot etal taht nam t'now dneb,
Tahw ylhtrae ecnatsmucric nac evas reh,
Morf tnemtnioppasid ni eht dne?

Eht ylno yaw ot gnirb mih revo,
Eht tsal tnemirepxe ot yrt,

Rehtehw a dnabsuh ro a revol,
Fi eh evah gnileef, si ot yrc.

(Nulls W, X, Z) — *Cary*

8. Key: *FRENZY*, at beginning, remaining letters in normal order.

Siht god dna nam ta tsrif erew sdneirf,
Tub nehw a euqip nageb,
Eht god, ot niag emos etavirp sdne,
Tnew dam dna tib eht nam.

Tub noos a rednow emac ot thgil
Taht dewohs eht seugor yeht deil:
Eht nam derevocer fo eht etib,
Eht god ti saw taht deid. — *Goldsmith*

9. Key: *VERYKIND*, at beginning, remaining letters in normal order.

Dna siht nediam ehs devil htiw on rehto thguoht
Naht ot evol dna eb devol yb em. (Nulls B, C) — *Poe*

10. Key: *MINTSAUCE*, at end, remaining letters in normal order.

Edirp hteog erofeb noitcurtsed dna na ythguah tirips erofeb a llaf. (Nulls P, A, C, E) — *Proverbs*

## *Group 14*

1. Substitution. Key: *YZTOMSHERIDAN*, remaining letters in normal order.

S'ereh ot eht remrahc esohw selpmid ew ezirp,
Won ot eht diam ohw sah enon, ris.
S'ereh ot eht lrig htiw a riap fo eulb seye,
Dna s'ereh ot eht hpmyn htiw tub eno, ris.

— *Sheridan*

2. Substitution. Key: *PROFLIGATE* in the middle of the alphabet, preceded by remaining letters, beginning *M*, and followed by remaining letters beginning *B*, in normal sequence.

O ereht saw na dlo pmacs dellac Llib
Taht devil no eht pot fo a llih
Eh sah ton neeb rebos
Ecnis tsal Rebotco
Dna I t'nod kniht taht eh reve lliw.

(Nulls J, K) — *Anon.*

3. Transposition. 4 × 13, A–4.[1]

Yreve nam si sa Nevaeh edam mih, dna semitemos a taerg laed esrow. — *Cervantes.*

4. Transposition. 5 × 11, E–4, nulls S, I, C.

Eht erom ew krow, eht erom ew yam,
Ti sekam on ecnereffid ot ruo yap.

— *War song of an unknown poet*

5. Substitution. Key: *METAPHYSIC*, at end, remaining letters in normal sequence.

Lla smees detcefni taht eht detcefni yps,
Sa lla skool wolley ot eht decidnuaj eye.

(Nulls S, I, C) — *Pope.*

6. Transposition. 5 × 12, G–2.

Tub ha, ehs evag em reven a kool
Rof reh seye erew delaes ot eht yloh koob.

(Nulls Q, E, D) — *Arnold*

7. Transposition. 5 × 10, F–3.

S'eh a loof ohw stel pils a drib ni eht dnah rof a drib ni eht hsub. — *Plutarch*

8. Transposition. 10 × 8, F–1.

Gnol oga a nam fo eht dlrow saw denifed sa a nam ohw ni yreve suoires sisirc si ylbairavni gnorw. (Nulls S, A, D) — *Anon.*

[1] This is a reference to the routing table on pages 41–43.

9. Substitution. Key: *PRESUMABLY*, at beginning, remaining letters in normal order.

Eh taht thah efiw dna nerdlihc htah nevig segatsoh ot enutrof, rof yeht era stnemidepmi ot taerg sesirpretne rehtie fo eutriv ro feihcsim. (Null z) — *Bacon*

10. Substitution. Key: *IMPERSONAL*, remaining letters in reverse order.

S'taht eht esiw hsurht. Eh sgnis hcae gnos eciwt revo
Tsel uoy dluohs kniht eh reven dluoc erutpacer
Eht tsrif enif sselerac erutpar.

(Nulls Y, Z) — *Browning*

## *15. The Task of Sisyphus*

Horizontal key word, *LACHRYMOSE*. Vigenère table (see page 71).

Vertical key word, *CAD*.

Eht rettel ecneuqerf fo siht txet si ylraen lamron. Eht rettel E srucco yltneuqerf ni hcae fo eht eerht stebahpla; dna, neve os, ta tseb ti si ton ysae ot evlos. Enon tub eht tsom tneitap dna luferac deen epoh ot deeccus: enon tub a doog gniddolp rekrow, gnivol gnol robal, dluohs tpmetta ti. Doog eyb, raed redaer, dna doog kcul.

# APPENDIX A

## *Some Notes on the Enciphering of Japanese*

To transmit a cipher message in any language, the Morse code, or some analogue of it, must be used. The sounds of the spoken language must be alphabetically or syllabically represented. This alphabetizing is done in the case of Japanese by romanizing the message — that is, writing in roman letters, our familiar alphabet. For romanized Japanese, a frequency table of ideographs obviously becomes useless; it does not apply to sounds. Therefore, to understand the complexities in breaking enciphered Japanese, we must look further at the nature of the language. At first the Japanese attempted to use the Chinese ideographs that they borrowed for phonetic purposes. As the vocabulary grew this device proved to be impractical, and a syllabary or *kana* was introduced, so that abbreviated Chinese characters or groups of them could be treated phonetically for purposes of inflection. These *kana* marks are written directly beside the character. Uninflected words are expressed by the unadorned ideographs. But verbs are conjugated, as are also — though at first it is hard to conceive it — adjectives. An adjective may express both mood and tense. But more often than not the true stem ends in a consonant, which written Japanese has no way to reveal. In consequence, the *kana* throws little light on the structure of the adjective or verb. That it complicates the language is apparent when we consider the fact that "adjective and verb inflections run to more than 2,000 forms." As Harold A.

Mallice points out in the *Library Quarterly*, "*Kirashimeraru-bekarazare-domo* is the actual concessive tense of the oblique mood of the passive causative negative voice of the verb *kiru*, 'to cut'." Since the personal pronoun in our sense of the word is not used in Japanese, it means, 'I [you, he, she, it, we, you, they] ought [would, might, should, etc.] not have been caused to cut'."

Such an example is enough to make one wonder how even the Japanese themselves can read their written language. As a matter of fact, there are cases in which even the most erudite of them cannot read what has been written. A stranger's signature, for instance, is unintelligible, so that one must ask him to pronounce it, or write and ask him to spell it out. The same applies to place names. Among the hundreds of other peculiarities of the language are these: In Japanese, often a sentence has no subject — yet it may have two subjects, one logical and one grammatical. There are no inflections to denote degrees of comparison. And — characteristically — the Japanese have no word for 'yes' or 'no.'

From time to time movements have been started to dispense with ideographs and to use roman letters in their place. But except for the purposes of telegraphy, nothing has been accomplished towards this end.

## APPENDIX B

# *The Baconian Biliteral Cipher*

Bacon's biliteral cipher was designed to conceal messages in the pages of printed books. Two type faces must be used by the printer. The fonts must differ, but so slightly that the difference will not be noticed by the casual reader. However, for the ease and comfort of both the reader and the compositor, light and bold face letters have been used instead, in the illustration following the alphabet below:

*The Baconian Alphabet*

| | | | | | | | |
|---|---|---|---|---|---|---|---|
| A | AAAAA | G | AABBA | N | ABBAA | T | BAABA |
| B | AAAAB | H | AABBB | O | ABBAB | UV | BAABB |
| C | AAABA | IJ | ABAAA | P | ABBBA | W | BABAA |
| D | AAABB | K | ABAAB | Q | ABBBB | X | BABAB |
| E | AABAA | L | ABABA | R | BAAAA | Y | BABBA |
| F | AABAB | M | ABABB | S | BAAAB | Z | BABBB |

In enciphering (that is, printing), light face letters represent *A*'s; bold face, *B*'s. The first five letters of a cipher text, such as "Sile**n**ce is the v**i**rt**ue** o**f** f**oo**ls," will thus yield the first plain-text letter, the next five the second, and so on. A twenty-five–letter cipher text, such as we have below, will therefore encipher only five plain-text letters. Dividing our cipher message into five-letter groups, and placing our A–B letters under them according to type face, we therefore have:

| | | | | | |
|---|---|---|---|---|---|
| Cipher: | SILE**N** | CEIST | HEV**I**R | T**UE**O**F** | F**OO**LS |
| Key: | AAAAB | AAAAA | AAABA | ABBAB | ABBAA |

The key is then interpreted into plain text by the alphabet given above:

| Key: | AAAAB | AAAAA | AAABA | ABBAB | ABBAA |
|---|---|---|---|---|---|
| Plain text: | *B* | *A* | *C* | *O* | *N* |

An ardent Baconian, having found in this text the word BACON concealed by the biliteral cipher alphabet, would leap to the conclusion that the line was written by Francis Bacon, first Baron Verulam and Viscount St. Albans — and he would be quite right.

# APPENDIX C

## *Letter and Word Frequency*

### English

*Order of frequency of single letters:* E T O A N I : R S H : D L : C W U M : F Y G P B : V K : X Q J Z

*Order of frequency of digraphs:* th er on an re he in ed nd ha at en es of or nt ea ti to it st io le is ou ar as de rt ve

*Order of frequency of trigraphs:* the and tha ent ion tio for nde has nce edt tis oft sth men

*Order of frequency of most common doubles:* ss ee tt ff ll mm oo

*Order of frequency of initial letters:* T O A W B C D S F M R H I Y E G L N P U J K

*Order of frequency of final letters:* E S T D N R Y F L O G H A K M P U W

*One-letter words:* a, I, O.

*Most frequent two-letter words:* of, to, in, it, is, be, as, at, so, we, he, by, or, on, do, if, me, my, up, an, go, no, us, am

*Most frequent three-letter words:* the, and, for, are, but, not, you, all, any, can, had, her, was, one, our, out, day, get, has, him, his, how, man, new, now, old, see, two, way, who, boy, did, its, let, put, say, she, too, use

*Most frequent four-letter words:* that, with, have, this, will, your, from, they, know, want, been, good, much, some, time, very, when, come, here, just, like, long, make, many, more, only, over, such, take, than, them, well, were

## French[1]

*Order of frequency of single letters:* E N A S R I U T O L D C M P V F B G X H Q Y Z J K W

*Most common digraphs:* es en le de on ou nt re ne ed te em se er ar me an it et ie ti el ns ur

*Most common trigraphs:* ent ede les lle que ait eme ion eur ell sse est dan del men des tio ese ans ter ons qui ais ous

*Most frequent doubles:* ss ll ee nn tt ff cc rr mm pp

*One-letter words:* a, y, o

*Most common two-letter words:* au, ce, ci, de, du, en, et, il, je, la, le, ma, me, ne, ni, on, ou, sa, se, si, un

## German[1]

*Order of frequency of single letters:* E N R I S T U D A H G L O C M B Z F W K V P J Q X Y

*Most common digraphs:* en er ch de ge ei ie in ne be el te un st di un ue se au re he it ri tz

*Most common trigraphs:* ein ich den der ten cht sch che die ung gen und nen des ben rch

*Most frequent doubles:* ee tt ll ss dd mm nn

*Common two-letter words:* ab, am, an, da, er, es, ob, so, wo, im, in, um, zu, du, ja.

## Italian[1]

*Order of frequency of single letters:* E I A O R L N T S C D P U M G V H Z B F Q J K W X Y

[1] Adapted from *Elementary Cryptography and Cryptanalysis*, by Donald D. Milliken, New York University Bookstore, 1942. By courtesy of the author.

*Most common digraphs:* er es on re de di ti si el en la al nt ra co ta to le li an in io ar or

*Most common trigraphs:* che ere zio del que ari ato eco edi ide esi idi ero par nte sta men

*Most frequent doubles:* ll ss tt ee pp nn bb gg cc

*One-letter words:* e, a, i, o

*Most common two-letter words:* di, in, ha, ho

## SPANISH[1]

*Order of frequency of single letters:* E A O S R I N L D C T U P M Y Q G B H F V J Z K W X

*Most common digraphs:* es en el de la os ar ue ra re er as on st ad ai or ta co se ac ec ci ia

*Most common trigraphs:* que est ara ado aqu del cio nte osa ede per ist nei res sde

*Most frequent doubles:* ee ll rr aa ss cc dd nn

*One-letter words:* a, e, o, u, y

*Most common two-letter words:* en, la, de, lo, el, se

[1] Adapted from *Elementary Cryptography and Cryptanalysis*, by Donald D. Milliken, New York University Bookstore, 1942. By courtesy of the author.

# APPENDIX D

## *Selected Bibliography*


d'Agapeyeff, Alexander, *Codes and Ciphers*, Oxford University Press, London, 1939.

Candela, Rosario, *The Military Cipher of Commandant Bazeries*, Cardanus Press, New York, 1938.

Gaines, Helen Fouché, *Elementary Cryptanalysis*, American Photographic Publishing Co., Boston, 1939.

Givierge, Marcel, *Cours de Cryptographie*, Gerger-Levrault, Paris, 1932.

Hitt, Parker, *Manual for the Solution of Military Ciphers*, U. S. Army School Service, Fort Leavenworth, Kansas, 1918.

Klüber, Johann Ludwig, *Kryptographik*, J. G. Cotta, Tübingen, 1809.

Lange, André, and Soudart, E. A., *Traité de cryptographie*, F. Alcan, Paris, 1925.

Langie, André, *Cryptography*, translated by J. C. H. Macbeth, Constable & Co., Ltd., London, 1922.

Mansfield, Louis C. S., *Solutions of Codes and Ciphers*, A. Maclehose & Co., London, 1936.

Mansfield, Louis C. S., *One Hundred Problems in Cipher*, A. Maclehose & Co., London, 1936.

Pratt, Fletcher, *Secret and Urgent, The Story of Codes and Ciphers*, The Bobbs-Merrill Company, Indianapolis, 1939.

Yardley, Herbert, *The American Black Chamber*, Bobbs-Merrill, Indianapolis, 1931.

# APPENDIX E

## *Definitions*

ACROSTIC, a text, usually in verse, in which a set or several sets of letters, as the first, second, or last letter of a line, when read in order form a word, phrase, or sentence.

ALPHABET

*Blocked*, an alphabet inscribed in a geometrical pattern, such as a square, the rows and columns of which are numbered to determine the cipher substitute for the plain-text letters. *See* p. 17.

*Cipher*, an alphabet composed of substitutes for the letters of the normal alphabet; the alphabet in which the cipher text is written.

*Mixed*, an alphabet in which the normal sequence of the letters is not followed, the letters having been disarranged.

*Plain text*, the normal alphabet.

ANAGRAM, the change of a word, phrase, or sentence into another by transposing its letters; the word, phrase, or sentence so formed. Thus, *are* is an anagram for *ear*.

BILITERAL, consisting of two letters. Also, in cryptography, employing two kinds of letters or type faces to conceal the plain text.

CELL, one of the rectangular units that compose the geometrical patterns used in transposition encipherment.

CIPHER, a method of secret or cryptographic writing that systematically disarranges the normal sequence of the letters of a plain text; or that substitutes other letters, characters, or symbols for the normal alphabet; or that combines these two devices for attaining secrecy.

*Diagrammatic*, a transposition cipher that employs diagrams, pictures, sketches, photographs, etc., to conceal the plain text.

*Substitution*

*Multiple or Polyalphabetic*, a substitution cipher system that involves two or more cipher alphabets.

*Simple or Monoalphabetic*, a substitution cipher system that involves the use of only one cipher alphabet.

*Transposition*, a cipher system in which the letters of the plain text are systematically disarranged by means of a key, or pattern.

CODE, (1) a system of signals for communication by telegraph, semaphore, etc.; (2) a cryptographic system by which groups of letters (usually five) are substituted for syllables, words, phrases, or sentences. *See* One-part code; Two-part code.

CRYPTANALYSIS, the science of deciphering (by analysis and deduction) of cryptograms, without prior knowledge of the keys or methods by which the plain texts were enciphered or encoded.

CRYPTANALYST, a person versed in deciphering or decoding by cryptanalysis.

CRYPTANALYZE, to decode or decipher a cryptogram by cryptanalysis.

CRYPTOGRAM, a text in code or cipher.

CRYPTOGRAPH, a mechanical device for enciphering and deciphering.

CRYPTOGRAPHY, the science of secret communication.

DECIPHER, to convert an enciphered text into a plain text.

DECODE, to convert an encoded text into a plain text.

DIGRAPH, a group of two letters.

DUMMIES, see *Nulls*

ENCIPHER, to convert a plain text into a cipher text.

ENCIPHERMENT, a text in cipher (1) formal, in which the letters, numerals or symbols of the cipher text are written in arbitrary group lengths, usually five units; (2) informal, one in which the length of each word in the plain text is preserved in the cipher text.

ENCODE, to convert a plain text into a cryptographic text by means of a code book.

FIGURE, see *Pattern*
FORMAL ENCIPHERMENT, see *Encipherment (1)*

GRILLE, a paper or cardboard, etc., with apertures or cells through which the secret message can be read after the grille has been properly placed over the text, letter, or composition, etc., in which the hidden message has been written.

IDIOGRAPH, a pictorial representation symbolizing a thing or idea of a thing, and not the name of it.
INFORMAL ENCIPHERMENT, see *Encipherment* (2)

KANA, the Japanese system of syllabic writing.
KEY, (1) a word, phrase, sentence, or number, etc., agreed upon by correspondents, that determines the steps to be followed in enciphering and deciphering; (2) a cipher alphabet, *q.v.*

MONOALPHABETIC SUBSTITUTION, see *Cipher, substitution, simple*
MULTIPLE-ALPHABET SUBSTITUTION, same as *Multiple substitution*
MULTIPLE SUBSTITUTION, see *Cipher, substitution, multiple*

NULLS, numerals, letters, or symbols of no significance, placed in a text either to complete a group or fill out a pattern or to make it more difficult for a cryptanalyst to discover the plain text.

ONE-PART CODE, a code book in which the plain-text words, phrases, and sentences are arranged in alphabetical order with the equivalent code groups, also in alphabetical order, beside them, so as to serve both for encoding and decoding.

PALINDROME, a word, verse, or sentence that reads the same from left to right as it does from right to left. Thus: *Anna. Lewd did I live, & evil I did dwel* (John Taylor).
PATTERN, the geometrical form in which the text is written in transposition encipherments.
POLYALPHABETIC SUBSTITUTION, see *Cipher, substitution, multiple*

POLYGRAPH SUBSTITUTION, the substitution of groups of letters or numbers integrally (as a group) for groups of letters in the plain text.

POLYGRAPH TRANSPOSITION, the transposing of groups of letters (two or more) integrally.

POLYLITERAL SUBSTITUTION, see *Polygraph substitution*

POLYLITERAL TRANSPOSITION, see *Polygraph transposition*

ROUTE, the order or sequence in which cells (*q.v.*) are selected in the geometrical pattern (*q.v.*) in transposition encipherment.

TRIGRAPH, a group of three letters.

TWO-PART CODE, a code book with two sections: an *encoding* section in which the plain-text words, phrases, etc., are arranged alphabetically with the code groups beside them, not alphabetically arranged; and a *decoding* section in which the code groups are alphabetically arranged but their meanings are not.

VARIANTS, two or more letters or characters that represent plain-text letters.

# *Index*

A CATALOG OF SELECTED

# DOVER BOOKS

IN ALL FIELDS OF INTEREST

# A CATALOG OF SELECTED DOVER BOOKS IN ALL FIELDS OF INTEREST

100 BEST-LOVED POEMS, Edited by Philip Smith. "The Passionate Shepherd to His Love," "Shall I compare thee to a summer's day?" "Death, be not proud," "The Raven," "The Road Not Taken," plus works by Blake, Wordsworth, Byron, Shelley, Keats, many others. 96pp. 5³⁄₁₆ x 8¼. 0-486-28553-7

100 SMALL HOUSES OF THE THIRTIES, Brown-Blodgett Company. Exterior photographs and floor plans for 100 charming structures. Illustrations of models accompanied by descriptions of interiors, color schemes, closet space, and other amenities. 200 illustrations. 112pp. 8⅜ x 11. 0-486-44131-8

1000 TURN-OF-THE-CENTURY HOUSES: With Illustrations and Floor Plans, Herbert C. Chivers. Reproduced from a rare edition, this showcase of homes ranges from cottages and bungalows to sprawling mansions. Each house is meticulously illustrated and accompanied by complete floor plans. 256pp. 9⅜ x 12¼. 0-486-45596-3

101 GREAT AMERICAN POEMS, Edited by The American Poetry & Literacy Project. Rich treasury of verse from the 19th and 20th centuries includes works by Edgar Allan Poe, Robert Frost, Walt Whitman, Langston Hughes, Emily Dickinson, T. S. Eliot, other notables. 96pp. 5³⁄₁₆ x 8¼. 0-486-40158-8

101 GREAT SAMURAI PRINTS, Utagawa Kuniyoshi. Kuniyoshi was a master of the warrior woodblock print — and these 18th-century illustrations represent the pinnacle of his craft. Full-color portraits of renowned Japanese samurais pulse with movement, passion, and remarkably fine detail. 112pp. 8⅜ x 11. 0-486-46523-3

ABC OF BALLET, Janet Grosser. Clearly worded, abundantly illustrated little guide defines basic ballet-related terms: arabesque, battement, pas de chat, relevé, sissonne, many others. Pronunciation guide included. Excellent primer. 48pp. 4³⁄₁₆ x 5¾. 0-486-40871-X

ACCESSORIES OF DRESS: An Illustrated Encyclopedia, Katherine Lester and Bess Viola Oerke. Illustrations of hats, veils, wigs, cravats, shawls, shoes, gloves, and other accessories enhance an engaging commentary that reveals the humor and charm of the many-sided story of accessorized apparel. 644 figures and 59 plates. 608pp. 6 ⅛ x 9¼. 0-486-43378-1

ADVENTURES OF HUCKLEBERRY FINN, Mark Twain. Join Huck and Jim as their boyhood adventures along the Mississippi River lead them into a world of excitement, danger, and self-discovery. Humorous narrative, lyrical descriptions of the Mississippi valley, and memorable characters. 224pp. 5³⁄₁₆ x 8¼. 0-486-28061-6

ALICE STARMORE'S BOOK OF FAIR ISLE KNITTING, Alice Starmore. A noted designer from the region of Scotland's Fair Isle explores the history and techniques of this distinctive, stranded-color knitting style and provides copious illustrated instructions for 14 original knitwear designs. 208pp. 8⅜ x 10⅞. 0-486-47218-3

**Browse over 9,000 books at www.doverpublications.com**

THE BATTLES THAT CHANGED HISTORY, Fletcher Pratt. Historian profiles 16 crucial conflicts, ancient to modern, that changed the course of Western civilization. Gripping accounts of battles led by Alexander the Great, Joan of Arc, Ulysses S. Grant, other commanders. 27 maps. 352pp. 5⅜ x 8½. 0-486-41129-X

BEETHOVEN'S LETTERS, Ludwig van Beethoven. Edited by Dr. A. C. Kalischer. Features 457 letters to fellow musicians, friends, greats, patrons, and literary men. Reveals musical thoughts, quirks of personality, insights, and daily events. Includes 15 plates. 410pp. 5⅜ x 8½. 0-486-22769-3

BERNICE BOBS HER HAIR AND OTHER STORIES, F. Scott Fitzgerald. This brilliant anthology includes 6 of Fitzgerald's most popular stories: "The Diamond as Big as the Ritz," the title tale, "The Offshore Pirate," "The Ice Palace," "The Jelly Bean," and "May Day." 176pp. 5⅜ x 8½. 0-486-47049-0

BESLER'S BOOK OF FLOWERS AND PLANTS: 73 Full-Color Plates from Hortus Eystettensis, 1613, Basilius Besler. Here is a selection of magnificent plates from the *Hortus Eystettensis,* which vividly illustrated and identified the plants, flowers, and trees that thrived in the legendary German garden at Eichstätt. 80pp. 8⅜ x 11. 0-486-46005-3

THE BOOK OF KELLS, Edited by Blanche Cirker. Painstakingly reproduced from a rare facsimile edition, this volume contains full-page decorations, portraits, illustrations, plus a sampling of textual leaves with exquisite calligraphy and ornamentation. 32 full-color illustrations. 32pp. 9⅜ x 12¼. 0-486-24345-1

THE BOOK OF THE CROSSBOW: With an Additional Section on Catapults and Other Siege Engines, Ralph Payne-Gallwey. Fascinating study traces history and use of crossbow as military and sporting weapon, from Middle Ages to modern times. Also covers related weapons: balistas, catapults, Turkish bows, more. Over 240 illustrations. 400pp. 7¼ x 10⅛. 0-486-28720-3

THE BUNGALOW BOOK: Floor Plans and Photos of 112 Houses, 1910, Henry L. Wilson. Here are 112 of the most popular and economic blueprints of the early 20th century — plus an illustration or photograph of each completed house. A wonderful time capsule that still offers a wealth of valuable insights. 160pp. 8⅜ x 11. 0-486-45104-6

THE CALL OF THE WILD, Jack London. A classic novel of adventure, drawn from London's own experiences as a Klondike adventurer, relating the story of a heroic dog caught in the brutal life of the Alaska Gold Rush. Note. 64pp. 5³⁄₁₆ x 8¼. 0-486-26472-6

CANDIDE, Voltaire. Edited by Francois-Marie Arouet. One of the world's great satires since its first publication in 1759. Witty, caustic skewering of romance, science, philosophy, religion, government — nearly all human ideals and institutions. 112pp. 5³⁄₁₆ x 8¼. 0-486-26689-3

CELEBRATED IN THEIR TIME: Photographic Portraits from the George Grantham Bain Collection, Edited by Amy Pastan. With an Introduction by Michael Carlebach. Remarkable portrait gallery features 112 rare images of Albert Einstein, Charlie Chaplin, the Wright Brothers, Henry Ford, and other luminaries from the worlds of politics, art, entertainment, and industry. 128pp. 8⅜ x 11. 0-486-46754-6

CHARIOTS FOR APOLLO: The NASA History of Manned Lunar Spacecraft to 1969, Courtney G. Brooks, James M. Grimwood, and Loyd S. Swenson, Jr. This illustrated history by a trio of experts is the definitive reference on the Apollo spacecraft and lunar modules. It traces the vehicles' design, development, and operation in space. More than 100 photographs and illustrations. 576pp. 6¾ x 9¼. 0-486-46756-2

A CHRISTMAS CAROL, Charles Dickens. This engrossing tale relates Ebenezer Scrooge's ghostly journeys through Christmases past, present, and future and his ultimate transformation from a harsh and grasping old miser to a charitable and compassionate human being. 80pp. 5³⁄₁₆ x 8¼. 0-486-26865-9

COMMON SENSE, Thomas Paine. First published in January of 1776, this highly influential landmark document clearly and persuasively argued for American separation from Great Britain and paved the way for the Declaration of Independence. 64pp. 5³⁄₁₆ x 8¼. 0-486-29602-4

THE COMPLETE SHORT STORIES OF OSCAR WILDE, Oscar Wilde. Complete texts of "The Happy Prince and Other Tales," "A House of Pomegranates," "Lord Arthur Savile's Crime and Other Stories," "Poems in Prose," and "The Portrait of Mr. W. H." 208pp. 5³⁄₁₆ x 8¼. 0-486-45216-6

COMPLETE SONNETS, William Shakespeare. Over 150 exquisite poems deal with love, friendship, the tyranny of time, beauty's evanescence, death, and other themes in language of remarkable power, precision, and beauty. Glossary of archaic terms. 80pp. 5³⁄₁₆ x 8¼. 0-486-26686-9

THE COUNT OF MONTE CRISTO: Abridged Edition, Alexandre Dumas. Falsely accused of treason, Edmond Dantès is imprisoned in the bleak Chateau d'If. After a hair-raising escape, he launches an elaborate plot to extract a bitter revenge against those who betrayed him. 448pp. 5³⁄₁₆ x 8¼. 0-486-45643-9

CRAFTSMAN BUNGALOWS: Designs from the Pacific Northwest, Yoho & Merritt. This reprint of a rare catalog, showcasing the charming simplicity and cozy style of Craftsman bungalows, is filled with photos of completed homes, plus floor plans and estimated costs. An indispensable resource for architects, historians, and illustrators. 112pp. 10 x 7. 0-486-46875-5

CRAFTSMAN BUNGALOWS: 59 Homes from "The Craftsman," Edited by Gustav Stickley. Best and most attractive designs from Arts and Crafts Movement publication — 1903–1916 — includes sketches, photographs of homes, floor plans, descriptive text. 128pp. 8¼ x 11. 0-486-25829-7

CRIME AND PUNISHMENT, Fyodor Dostoyevsky. Translated by Constance Garnett. Supreme masterpiece tells the story of Raskolnikov, a student tormented by his own thoughts after he murders an old woman. Overwhelmed by guilt and terror, he confesses and goes to prison. 480pp. 5³⁄₁₆ x 8¼. 0-486-41587-2

THE DECLARATION OF INDEPENDENCE AND OTHER GREAT DOCUMENTS OF AMERICAN HISTORY: 1775-1865, Edited by John Grafton. Thirteen compelling and influential documents: Henry's "Give Me Liberty or Give Me Death," Declaration of Independence, The Constitution, Washington's First Inaugural Address, The Monroe Doctrine, The Emancipation Proclamation, Gettysburg Address, more. 64pp. 5³⁄₁₆ x 8¼. 0-486-41124-9

THE DESERT AND THE SOWN: Travels in Palestine and Syria, Gertrude Bell. "The female Lawrence of Arabia," Gertrude Bell wrote captivating, perceptive accounts of her travels in the Middle East. This intriguing narrative, accompanied by 160 photos, traces her 1905 sojourn in Lebanon, Syria, and Palestine. 368pp. 5⅜ x 8½. 0-486-46876-3

A DOLL'S HOUSE, Henrik Ibsen. Ibsen's best-known play displays his genius for realistic prose drama. An expression of women's rights, the play climaxes when the central character, Nora, rejects a smothering marriage and life in "a doll's house." 80pp. 5³⁄₁₆ x 8¼. 0-486-27062-9

DOOMED SHIPS: Great Ocean Liner Disasters, William H. Miller, Jr. Nearly 200 photographs, many from private collections, highlight tales of some of the vessels whose pleasure cruises ended in catastrophe: the *Morro Castle, Normandie, Andrea Doria, Europa,* and many others. 128pp. 8⅞ x 11¾. 0-486-45366-9

THE DORÉ BIBLE ILLUSTRATIONS, Gustave Doré. Detailed plates from the Bible: the Creation scenes, Adam and Eve, horrifying visions of the Flood, the battle sequences with their monumental crowds, depictions of the life of Jesus, 241 plates in all. 241pp. 9 x 12. 0-486-23004-X

DRAWING DRAPERY FROM HEAD TO TOE, Cliff Young. Expert guidance on how to draw shirts, pants, skirts, gloves, hats, and coats on the human figure, including folds in relation to the body, pull and crush, action folds, creases, more. Over 200 drawings. 48pp. 8¼ x 11. 0-486-45591-2

DUBLINERS, James Joyce. A fine and accessible introduction to the work of one of the 20th century's most influential writers, this collection features 15 tales, including a masterpiece of the short-story genre, "The Dead." 160pp. 5³⁄₁₆ x 8¼. 0-486-26870-5

EASY-TO-MAKE POP-UPS, Joan Irvine. Illustrated by Barbara Reid. Dozens of wonderful ideas for three-dimensional paper fun — from holiday greeting cards with moving parts to a pop-up menagerie. Easy-to-follow, illustrated instructions for more than 30 projects. 299 black-and-white illustrations. 96pp. 8⅜ x 11. 0-486-44622-0

EASY-TO-MAKE STORYBOOK DOLLS: A "Novel" Approach to Cloth Dollmaking, Sherralyn St. Clair. Favorite fictional characters come alive in this unique beginner's dollmaking guide. Includes patterns for Pollyanna, Dorothy from *The Wonderful Wizard of Oz,* Mary of *The Secret Garden,* plus easy-to-follow instructions, 263 black-and-white illustrations, and an 8-page color insert. 112pp. 8¼ x 11. 0-486-47360-0

EINSTEIN'S ESSAYS IN SCIENCE, Albert Einstein. Speeches and essays in accessible, everyday language profile influential physicists such as Niels Bohr and Isaac Newton. They also explore areas of physics to which the author made major contributions. 128pp. 5 x 8. 0-486-47011-3

EL DORADO: Further Adventures of the Scarlet Pimpernel, Baroness Orczy. A popular sequel to *The Scarlet Pimpernel,* this suspenseful story recounts the Pimpernel's attempts to rescue the Dauphin from imprisonment during the French Revolution. An irresistible blend of intrigue, period detail, and vibrant characterizations. 352pp. 5³⁄₁₆ x 8¼. 0-486-44026-5

ELEGANT SMALL HOMES OF THE TWENTIES: 99 Designs from a Competition, Chicago Tribune. Nearly 100 designs for five- and six-room houses feature New England and Southern colonials, Normandy cottages, stately Italianate dwellings, and other fascinating snapshots of American domestic architecture of the 1920s. 112pp. 9 x 12. 0-486-46910-7

THE ELEMENTS OF STYLE: The Original Edition, William Strunk, Jr. This is the book that generations of writers have relied upon for timeless advice on grammar, diction, syntax, and other essentials. In concise terms, it identifies the principal requirements of proper style and common errors. 64pp. 5⅜ x 8½. 0-486-44798-7

THE ELUSIVE PIMPERNEL, Baroness Orczy. Robespierre's revolutionaries find their wicked schemes thwarted by the heroic Pimpernel — Sir Percival Blakeney. In this thrilling sequel, Chauvelin devises a plot to eliminate the Pimpernel and his wife. 272pp. 5³⁄₁₆ x 8¼. 0-486-45464-9

AN ENCYCLOPEDIA OF BATTLES: Accounts of Over 1,560 Battles from 1479 B.C. to the Present, David Eggenberger. Essential details of every major battle in recorded history from the first battle of Megiddo in 1479 B.C. to Grenada in 1984. List of battle maps. 99 illustrations. 544pp. 6½ x 9¼. 0-486-24913-1

ENCYCLOPEDIA OF EMBROIDERY STITCHES, INCLUDING CREWEL, Marion Nichols. Precise explanations and instructions, clearly illustrated, on how to work chain, back, cross, knotted, woven stitches, and many more — 178 in all, including Cable Outline, Whipped Satin, and Eyelet Buttonhole. Over 1400 illustrations. 219pp. 8⅜ x 11¼. 0-486-22929-7

ENTER JEEVES: 15 Early Stories, P. G. Wodehouse. Splendid collection contains first 8 stories featuring Bertie Wooster, the deliciously dim aristocrat and Jeeves, his brainy, imperturbable manservant. Also, the complete Reggie Pepper (Bertie's prototype) series. 288pp. 5⅜ x 8½. 0-486-29717-9

ERIC SLOANE'S AMERICA: Paintings in Oil, Michael Wigley. With a Foreword by Mimi Sloane. Eric Sloane's evocative oils of America's landscape and material culture shimmer with immense historical and nostalgic appeal. This original hardcover collection gathers nearly a hundred of his finest paintings, with subjects ranging from New England to the American Southwest. 128pp. 10⅝ x 9. 0-486-46525-X

ETHAN FROME, Edith Wharton. Classic story of wasted lives, set against a bleak New England background. Superbly delineated characters in a hauntingly grim tale of thwarted love. Considered by many to be Wharton's masterpiece. 96pp. 5³⁄₁₆ x 8 ¼. 0-486-26690-7

THE EVERLASTING MAN, G. K. Chesterton. Chesterton's view of Christianity — as a blend of philosophy and mythology, satisfying intellect and spirit — applies to his brilliant book, which appeals to readers' heads as well as their hearts. 288pp. 5⅜ x 8½. 0-486-46036-3

THE FIELD AND FOREST HANDY BOOK, Daniel Beard. Written by a co-founder of the Boy Scouts, this appealing guide offers illustrated instructions for building kites, birdhouses, boats, igloos, and other fun projects, plus numerous helpful tips for campers. 448pp. 5³⁄₁₆ x 8¼. 0-486-46191-2

FINDING YOUR WAY WITHOUT MAP OR COMPASS, Harold Gatty. Useful, instructive manual shows would-be explorers, hikers, bikers, scouts, sailors, and survivalists how to find their way outdoors by observing animals, weather patterns, shifting sands, and other elements of nature. 288pp. 5⅜ x 8½. 0-486-40613-X

FIRST FRENCH READER: A Beginner's Dual-Language Book, Edited and Translated by Stanley Appelbaum. This anthology introduces 50 legendary writers — Voltaire, Balzac, Baudelaire, Proust, more — through passages from *The Red and the Black, Les Misérables, Madame Bovary,* and other classics. Original French text plus English translation on facing pages. 240pp. 5⅜ x 8½. 0-486-46178-5

FIRST GERMAN READER: A Beginner's Dual-Language Book, Edited by Harry Steinhauer. Specially chosen for their power to evoke German life and culture, these short, simple readings include poems, stories, essays, and anecdotes by Goethe, Hesse, Heine, Schiller, and others. 224pp. 5⅜ x 8½. 0-486-46179-3

FIRST SPANISH READER: A Beginner's Dual-Language Book, Angel Flores. Delightful stories, other material based on works of Don Juan Manuel, Luis Taboada, Ricardo Palma, other noted writers. Complete faithful English translations on facing pages. Exercises. 176pp. 5⅜ x 8½. 0-486-25810-6

FIVE ACRES AND INDEPENDENCE, Maurice G. Kains. Great back-to-the-land classic explains basics of self-sufficient farming. The one book to get. 95 illustrations. 397pp. 5⅜ x 8½. 0-486-20974-1

FLAGG'S SMALL HOUSES: Their Economic Design and Construction, 1922, Ernest Flagg. Although most famous for his skyscrapers, Flagg was also a proponent of the well-designed single-family dwelling. His classic treatise features innovations that save space, materials, and cost. 526 illustrations. 160pp. 9⅜ x 12¼. 0-486-45197-6

FLATLAND: A Romance of Many Dimensions, Edwin A. Abbott. Classic of science (and mathematical) fiction — charmingly illustrated by the author — describes the adventures of A. Square, a resident of Flatland, in Spaceland (three dimensions), Lineland (one dimension), and Pointland (no dimensions). 96pp. 5$^{3}/_{16}$ x 8¼. 0-486-27263-X

FRANKENSTEIN, Mary Shelley. The story of Victor Frankenstein's monstrous creation and the havoc it caused has enthralled generations of readers and inspired countless writers of horror and suspense. With the author's own 1831 introduction. 176pp. 5$^{3}/_{16}$ x 8¼. 0-486-28211-2

THE GARGOYLE BOOK: 572 Examples from Gothic Architecture, Lester Burbank Bridaham. Dispelling the conventional wisdom that French Gothic architectural flourishes were born of despair or gloom, Bridaham reveals the whimsical nature of these creations and the ingenious artisans who made them. 572 illustrations. 224pp. 8⅜ x 11. 0-486-44754-5

THE GIFT OF THE MAGI AND OTHER SHORT STORIES, O. Henry. Sixteen captivating stories by one of America's most popular storytellers. Included are such classics as "The Gift of the Magi," "The Last Leaf," and "The Ransom of Red Chief." Publisher's Note. 96pp. 5$^{3}/_{16}$ x 8¼. 0-486-27061-0

THE GOETHE TREASURY: Selected Prose and Poetry, Johann Wolfgang von Goethe. Edited, Selected, and with an Introduction by Thomas Mann. In addition to his lyric poetry, Goethe wrote travel sketches, autobiographical studies, essays, letters, and proverbs in rhyme and prose. This collection presents outstanding examples from each genre. 368pp. 5⅜ x 8½. 0-486-44780-4

GREAT EXPECTATIONS, Charles Dickens. Orphaned Pip is apprenticed to the dirty work of the forge but dreams of becoming a gentleman — and one day finds himself in possession of "great expectations." Dickens' finest novel. 400pp. 5$^{3}/_{16}$ x 8¼. 0-486-41586-4

GREAT WRITERS ON THE ART OF FICTION: From Mark Twain to Joyce Carol Oates, Edited by James Daley. An indispensable source of advice and inspiration, this anthology features essays by Henry James, Kate Chopin, Willa Cather, Sinclair Lewis, Jack London, Raymond Chandler, Raymond Carver, Eudora Welty, and Kurt Vonnegut, Jr. 192pp. 5⅜ x 8½. 0-486-45128-3

HAMLET, William Shakespeare. The quintessential Shakespearean tragedy, whose highly charged confrontations and anguished soliloquies probe depths of human feeling rarely sounded in any art. Reprinted from an authoritative British edition complete with illuminating footnotes. 128pp. 5$^{3}/_{16}$ x 8¼. 0-486-27278-8

THE HAUNTED HOUSE, Charles Dickens. A Yuletide gathering in an eerie country retreat provides the backdrop for Dickens and his friends — including Elizabeth Gaskell and Wilkie Collins — who take turns spinning supernatural yarns. 144pp. 5⅜ x 8½. 0-486-46309-5

HEART OF DARKNESS, Joseph Conrad. Dark allegory of a journey up the Congo River and the narrator's encounter with the mysterious Mr. Kurtz. Masterly blend of adventure, character study, psychological penetration. For many, Conrad's finest, most enigmatic story. 80pp. 5³⁄₁₆ x 8¼. 0-486-26464-5

HENSON AT THE NORTH POLE, Matthew A. Henson. This thrilling memoir by the heroic African-American who was Peary's companion through two decades of Arctic exploration recounts a tale of danger, courage, and determination. "Fascinating and exciting." — *Commonweal.* 128pp. 5⅜ x 8½. 0-486-45472-X

HISTORIC COSTUMES AND HOW TO MAKE THEM, Mary Fernald and E. Shenton. Practical, informative guidebook shows how to create everything from short tunics worn by Saxon men in the fifth century to a lady's bustle dress of the late 1800s. 81 illustrations. 176pp. 5⅜ x 8½. 0-486-44906-8

THE HOUND OF THE BASKERVILLES, Arthur Conan Doyle. A deadly curse in the form of a legendary ferocious beast continues to claim its victims from the Baskerville family until Holmes and Watson intervene. Often called the best detective story ever written. 128pp. 5³⁄₁₆ x 8¼. 0-486-28214-7

THE HOUSE BEHIND THE CEDARS, Charles W. Chesnutt. Originally published in 1900, this groundbreaking novel by a distinguished African-American author recounts the drama of a brother and sister who "pass for white" during the dangerous days of Reconstruction. 208pp. 5⅜ x 8½. 0-486-46144-0

THE HUMAN FIGURE IN MOTION, Eadweard Muybridge. The 4,789 photographs in this definitive selection show the human figure — models almost all undraped — engaged in over 160 different types of action: running, climbing stairs, etc. 390pp. 7⅞ x 10⅝. 0-486-20204-6

THE IMPORTANCE OF BEING EARNEST, Oscar Wilde. Wilde's witty and buoyant comedy of manners, filled with some of literature's most famous epigrams, reprinted from an authoritative British edition. Considered Wilde's most perfect work. 64pp. 5³⁄₁₆ x 8¼. 0-486-26478-5

THE INFERNO, Dante Alighieri. Translated and with notes by Henry Wadsworth Longfellow. The first stop on Dante's famous journey from Hell to Purgatory to Paradise, this 14th-century allegorical poem blends vivid and shocking imagery with graceful lyricism. Translated by the beloved 19th-century poet, Henry Wadsworth Longfellow. 256pp. 5³⁄₁₆ x 8¼. 0-486-44288-8

JANE EYRE, Charlotte Brontë. Written in 1847, *Jane Eyre* tells the tale of an orphan girl's progress from the custody of cruel relatives to an oppressive boarding school and its culmination in a troubled career as a governess. 448pp. 5³⁄₁₆ x 8¼. 0-486-42449-9

JAPANESE WOODBLOCK FLOWER PRINTS, Tanigami Kônan. Extraordinary collection of Japanese woodblock prints by a well-known artist features 120 plates in brilliant color. Realistic images from a rare edition include daffodils, tulips, and other familiar and unusual flowers. 128pp. 11 x 8¼. 0-486-46442-3

JEWELRY MAKING AND DESIGN, Augustus F. Rose and Antonio Cirino. Professional secrets of jewelry making are revealed in a thorough, practical guide. Over 200 illustrations. 306pp. 5⅜ x 8½. 0-486-21750-7

JULIUS CAESAR, William Shakespeare. Great tragedy based on Plutarch's account of the lives of Brutus, Julius Caesar and Mark Antony. Evil plotting, ringing oratory, high tragedy with Shakespeare's incomparable insight, dramatic power. Explanatory footnotes. 96pp. 5³⁄₁₆ x 8¼. 0-486-26876-4

THE METAMORPHOSIS AND OTHER STORIES, Franz Kafka. Excellent new English translations of title story (considered by many critics Kafka's most perfect work), plus "The Judgment," "In the Penal Colony," "A Country Doctor," and "A Report to an Academy." Note. 96pp. 5³⁄₁₆ x 8¼. 0-486-29030-1

MICROSCOPIC ART FORMS FROM THE PLANT WORLD, R. Anheisser. From undulating curves to complex geometrics, a world of fascinating images abound in this classic, illustrated survey of microscopic plants. Features 400 detailed illustrations of nature's minute but magnificent handiwork. The accompanying CD-ROM includes all of the images in the book. 128pp. 9 x 9. 0-486-46013-4

A MIDSUMMER NIGHT'S DREAM, William Shakespeare. Among the most popular of Shakespeare's comedies, this enchanting play humorously celebrates the vagaries of love as it focuses upon the intertwined romances of several pairs of lovers. Explanatory footnotes. 80pp. 5³⁄₁₆ x 8¼. 0-486-27067-X

THE MONEY CHANGERS, Upton Sinclair. Originally published in 1908, this cautionary novel from the author of *The Jungle* explores corruption within the American system as a group of power brokers joins forces for personal gain, triggering a crash on Wall Street. 192pp. 5⅜ x 8½. 0-486-46917-4

THE MOST POPULAR HOMES OF THE TWENTIES, William A. Radford. With a New Introduction by Daniel D. Reiff. Based on a rare 1925 catalog, this architectural showcase features floor plans, construction details, and photos of 26 homes, plus articles on entrances, porches, garages, and more. 250 illustrations, 21 color plates. 176pp. 8⅜ x 11. 0-486-47028-8

MY 66 YEARS IN THE BIG LEAGUES, Connie Mack. With a New Introduction by Rich Westcott. A Founding Father of modern baseball, Mack holds the record for most wins — and losses — by a major league manager. Enhanced by 70 photographs, his warmhearted autobiography is populated by many legends of the game. 288pp. 5⅜ x 8½. 0-486-47184-5

NARRATIVE OF THE LIFE OF FREDERICK DOUGLASS, Frederick Douglass. Douglass's graphic depictions of slavery, harrowing escape to freedom, and life as a newspaper editor, eloquent orator, and impassioned abolitionist. 96pp. 5³⁄₁₆ x 8¼. 0-486-28499-9

THE NIGHTLESS CITY: Geisha and Courtesan Life in Old Tokyo, J. E. de Becker. This unsurpassed study from 100 years ago ventured into Tokyo's red-light district to survey geisha and courtesan life and offer meticulous descriptions of training, dress, social hierarchy, and erotic practices. 49 black-and-white illustrations; 2 maps. 496pp. 5⅜ x 8½. 0-486-45563-7

THE ODYSSEY, Homer. Excellent prose translation of ancient epic recounts adventures of the homeward-bound Odysseus. Fantastic cast of gods, giants, cannibals, sirens, other supernatural creatures — true classic of Western literature. 256pp. 5³⁄₁₆ x 8¼. 0-486-40654-7

OEDIPUS REX, Sophocles. Landmark of Western drama concerns the catastrophe that ensues when King Oedipus discovers he has inadvertently killed his father and married his mother. Masterly construction, dramatic irony. Explanatory footnotes. 64pp. 5³⁄₁₆ x 8¼. 0-486-26877-2

ONCE UPON A TIME: The Way America Was, Eric Sloane. Nostalgic text and drawings brim with gentle philosophies and descriptions of how we used to live — self-sufficiently — on the land, in homes, and among the things built by hand. 44 line illustrations. 64pp. 8⅜ x 11. 0-486-44411-2

THE RED BADGE OF COURAGE, Stephen Crane. Amid the nightmarish chaos of a Civil War battle, a young soldier discovers courage, humility, and, perhaps, wisdom. Uncanny re-creation of actual combat. Enduring landmark of American fiction. 112pp. 5³⁄₁₆ x 8¼. 0-486-26465-3

RELATIVITY SIMPLY EXPLAINED, Martin Gardner. One of the subject's clearest, most entertaining introductions offers lucid explanations of special and general theories of relativity, gravity, and spacetime, models of the universe, and more. 100 illustrations. 224pp. 5⅜ x 8½. 0-486-29315-7

REMBRANDT DRAWINGS: 116 Masterpieces in Original Color, Rembrandt van Rijn. This deluxe hardcover edition features drawings from throughout the Dutch master's prolific career. Informative captions accompany these beautifully reproduced landscapes, biblical vignettes, figure studies, animal sketches, and portraits. 128pp. 8⅜ x 11. 0-486-46149-1

THE ROAD NOT TAKEN AND OTHER POEMS, Robert Frost. A treasury of Frost's most expressive verse. In addition to the title poem: "An Old Man's Winter Night," "In the Home Stretch," "Meeting and Passing," "Putting in the Seed," many more. All complete and unabridged. 64pp. 5³⁄₁₆ x 8¼. 0-486-27550-7

ROMEO AND JULIET, William Shakespeare. Tragic tale of star-crossed lovers, feuding families and timeless passion contains some of Shakespeare's most beautiful and lyrical love poetry. Complete, unabridged text with explanatory footnotes. 96pp. 5³⁄₁₆ x 8¼. 0-486-27557-4

SANDITON AND THE WATSONS: Austen's Unfinished Novels, Jane Austen. Two tantalizing incomplete stories revisit Austen's customary milieu of courtship and venture into new territory, amid guests at a seaside resort. Both are worth reading for pleasure and study. 112pp. 5⅜ x 8½. 0-486-45793-1

THE SCARLET LETTER, Nathaniel Hawthorne. With stark power and emotional depth, Hawthorne's masterpiece explores sin, guilt, and redemption in a story of adultery in the early days of the Massachusetts Colony. 192pp. 5³⁄₁₆ x 8¼. 0-486-28048-9

THE SEASONS OF AMERICA PAST, Eric Sloane. Seventy-five illustrations depict cider mills and presses, sleds, pumps, stump-pulling equipment, plows, and other elements of America's rural heritage. A section of old recipes and household hints adds additional color. 160pp. 8⅜ x 11. 0-486-44220-9

SELECTED CANTERBURY TALES, Geoffrey Chaucer. Delightful collection includes the General Prologue plus three of the most popular tales: "The Knight's Tale," "The Miller's Prologue and Tale," and "The Wife of Bath's Prologue and Tale." In modern English. 144pp. 5³⁄₁₆ x 8¼. 0-486-28241-4

SELECTED POEMS, Emily Dickinson. Over 100 best-known, best-loved poems by one of America's foremost poets, reprinted from authoritative early editions. No comparable edition at this price. Index of first lines. 64pp. 5³⁄₁₆ x 8¼. 0-486-26466-1

SIDDHARTHA, Hermann Hesse. Classic novel that has inspired generations of seekers. Blending Eastern mysticism and psychoanalysis, Hesse presents a strikingly original view of man and culture and the arduous process of self-discovery, reconciliation, harmony, and peace. 112pp. 5³⁄₁₆ x 8¼. 0-486-40653-9

SKETCHING OUTDOORS, Leonard Richmond. This guide offers beginners step-by-step demonstrations of how to depict clouds, trees, buildings, and other outdoor sights. Explanations of a variety of techniques include shading and constructional drawing. 48pp. 11 x 8¼. 0-486-46922-0

SMALL HOUSES OF THE FORTIES: With Illustrations and Floor Plans, Harold E. Group. 56 floor plans and elevations of houses that originally cost less than $15,000 to build. Recommended by financial institutions of the era, they range from Colonials to Cape Cods. 144pp. 8⅜ x 11. 0-486-45598-X

SOME CHINESE GHOSTS, Lafcadio Hearn. Rooted in ancient Chinese legends, these richly atmospheric supernatural tales are recounted by an expert in Oriental lore. Their originality, power, and literary charm will captivate readers of all ages. 96pp. 5⅜ x 8½. 0-486-46306-0

SONGS FOR THE OPEN ROAD: Poems of Travel and Adventure, Edited by The American Poetry & Literacy Project. More than 80 poems by 50 American and British masters celebrate real and metaphorical journeys. Poems by Whitman, Byron, Millay, Sandburg, Langston Hughes, Emily Dickinson, Robert Frost, Shelley, Tennyson, Yeats, many others. Note. 80pp. 5 3/16 x 8¼. 0-486-40646-6

SPOON RIVER ANTHOLOGY, Edgar Lee Masters. An American poetry classic, in which former citizens of a mythical midwestern town speak touchingly from the grave of the thwarted hopes and dreams of their lives. 144pp. 5 3/16 x 8¼. 0-486-27275-3

STAR LORE: Myths, Legends, and Facts, William Tyler Olcott. Captivating retellings of the origins and histories of ancient star groups include Pegasus, Ursa Major, Pleiades, signs of the zodiac, and other constellations. "Classic." — *Sky & Telescope*. 58 illustrations. 544pp. 5⅜ x 8½. 0-486-43581-4

THE STRANGE CASE OF DR. JEKYLL AND MR. HYDE, Robert Louis Stevenson. This intriguing novel, both fantasy thriller and moral allegory, depicts the struggle of two opposing personalities — one essentially good, the other evil — for the soul of one man. 64pp. 5 3/16 x 8¼. 0-486-26688-5

SURVIVAL HANDBOOK: The Official U.S. Army Guide, Department of the Army. This special edition of the Army field manual is geared toward civilians. An essential companion for campers and all lovers of the outdoors, it constitutes the most authoritative wilderness guide. 288pp. 5 3/16 x 8¼. 0-486-46184-X

A TALE OF TWO CITIES, Charles Dickens. Against the backdrop of the French Revolution, Dickens unfolds his masterpiece of drama, adventure, and romance about a man falsely accused of treason. Excitement and derring-do in the shadow of the guillotine. 304pp. 5 3/16 x 8¼. 0-486-40651-2

TEN PLAYS, Anton Chekhov. *The Sea Gull, Uncle Vanya, The Three Sisters, The Cherry Orchard,* and *Ivanov,* plus 5 one-act comedies: *The Anniversary, An Unwilling Martyr, The Wedding, The Bear,* and *The Proposal.* 336pp. 5 3/16 x 8¼. 0-486-46560-8

THE FLYING INN, G. K. Chesterton. Hilarious romp in which pub owner Humphrey Hump and friend take to the road in a donkey cart filled with rum and cheese, inveighing against Prohibition and other "oppressive forms of modernity." 320pp. 5⅜ x 8½. 0-486-41910-X

THIRTY YEARS THAT SHOOK PHYSICS: The Story of Quantum Theory, George Gamow. Lucid, accessible introduction to the influential theory of energy and matter features careful explanations of Dirac's anti-particles, Bohr's model of the atom, and much more. Numerous drawings. 1966 edition. 240pp. 5⅜ x 8½. 0-486-24895-X

TREASURE ISLAND, Robert Louis Stevenson. Classic adventure story of a perilous sea journey, a mutiny led by the infamous Long John Silver, and a lethal scramble for buried treasure — seen through the eyes of cabin boy Jim Hawkins. 160pp. 5 3/16 x 8¼. 0-486-27559-0